HEALING IS A
CHOICE
WORKBOOK

TEN DECISIONS THAT WILL TRANSFORM YOUR LIFE & TEN LIES THAT CAN PREVENT YOU FROM MAKING THEM

Stephen Arterburn, M. Ed.

with

Bill Martin

NELSON
A Division of Thomas
Since
www.thomasn

Published by Nelson Impact, a Division of Thomas Nelson, Inc., P.O. Box 141000, Nashville, Tennessee 37214.

Nelson Books titles may be purchased in bulk for educational, business, fund-raising, or sales promotional use. For information, please e-mail SpecialMarkets@ThomasNelson.com.

ISBN 1-4185-0194-8

Printed in the United States of America

05 06 07 08 09 PP 5 4 3 2 1

CONTENTS

CONTENTS

INTRODUCTION

LISTED BELOW ARE SOME QUESTIONS YOU MAY HAVE ABOUT THIS WORKBOOK:

What will the *Healing Is a Choice Workbook* do for me? This workbook will guide you through a study of the ten important choices that contribute to healing, and the ten lies that work against people in the healing process. It will challenge the reader to engage in introspection concerning the need for healing, and to develop a proactive approach to becoming well.

Is this workbook enough or do I also need the book, *Healing Is a Choice*? The book *Healing Is a Choice* contains all the primary and necessary information. The workbook is a companion text designed to reinforce the content and enhance your ability to assimilate and apply the truths found in the book.

The lessons look long. Do I need to work through everything in each one? *Healing Is a Choice* begins with an important premise and builds upon it throughout the text. Reading from the beginning to the end provides a thorough understanding of the subject and its applications. You need it all to receive the most benefit. The workbook is intended to reinforce the truths in the book and guide the reader toward application. If you neglect selected passages, you may experience some loss in application. Choose carefully.

How do I bring together a small group to go through this workbook? There is no greater learning environment than an interactive small group. If you share this book with friends and colleagues, you will probably discover a keen interest among them. The fact is that many people are in need of healing, or they certainly know people who are. Gathering some of them into a small group to study this book might be just the prescription that will change their lives.

How should I use the workbook? We will consider one chapter at a time. Reading it will give you the basic information. Using the workbook will provide reinforcement of the book's content through a variety of questions, exercises, and devotionals. Take time to complete them. Following this method will provide the greatest impact.

What is the structure of the book? *Healing Is a Choice* identifies and explains ten important healing choices that people can make as they seek healing. In contrast, it identifies ten big lies that hinder and derail healing. This contrasting style encourages an emphasis on the healing choices, while making us aware of the lies that would dissuade us from making choices that heal. In every case, healing is a choice in which God and man are involved. Healing is God's choice. Man's choice is to reject the lies that work against healing.

1

THE FIRST CHOICE:
The Choice to Connect Your Life

THE FIRST BIG LIE:
"All I need to heal is just God and me."

IF WE SENSE THAT WE ARE NOT WELL AND REALLY WANT TO recover, it is important that we connect with others. Whether it is a physician, a health practitioner, a counselor, or a trusted friend, the need to connect during the healing process is profound. A physician has the expertise to diagnose and prescribe medicine. A counselor can help us examine the emotional pain we often have and guide us toward the means of dealing with it, so that healing occurs. A friend stands solidly with us during illness; supporting, praying, helping, and most of all, caring.

In fact, connecting with friends in our time of illness or crisis is one way to fulfill God's purpose in relationships.

THE FIRST CHOICE:
The Important Choice to Connect Our Lives with Others

Key Scripture: *Carry each other's burdens, and in this way you will fulfill the law of Christ.*

—Galatians 6:2 NIV

The introduction to *Healing Is a Choice* makes the point: "At one time or another, every human being needs healing" (Introduction, page vii). It is a rare person who marches through life without being ill. Such folks are fortunate, because the more common human condition is that people get sick from time to time.

Typically, our illnesses are physical. We catch a cold, have a headache, or are down with the flu. Other illnesses, like high blood pressure and diabetes, do their damage "silently" without visible symptoms.

We can usually find effective medications and treatments to manage most of our physical illnesses. Medical treatment often speeds our healing. Frankly, we should be very thankful to live in a society where good medical service is available.

THINK ABOUT IT!

Medicine cannot benefit us unless we are willing to take it. The doctor can only prescribe the medicines we need. It is our choice to take them and experience the healing that results. In fact, every illness provides a number of choices for people. Most people feel just the opposite. They have a sense of being out of control during illness, but that is rarely the case. Rather, an ill person usually has many choices to make.

Exercise #1

Remember a time when you were ill. (If you've never been ill, think of a friend or a family member.) Try to remember how the illness began, what visits to the doctor were like, and what was required for you to ultimately be well. Can you recall how many choices you had during the entire experience of the illness?

List the decisions below, no matter how important or insignificant they seem.

Seven spaces have been provided, but you may add more.

(1) _____

(2) _____

(3) _____

(4) _____

(5) _____

(6) _____

(7) _____

CHOICES, CHOICES, CHOICES!

Were you surprised by the number of choices you had? Thinking it through usually reveals that we had far more choices than we imagined during the illness. An individual must choose whether to see a doctor or consult a different kind of medical expert. In most of the United States, people can select the doctor they will see. When physicians diagnose a problem and suggest treatment options, the patient is usually part of the discussion and can make choices regarding various treatment plans. He or she must decide whether to rest and recover or continue to work. As mentioned earlier, the doctor may prescribe medicine, but the ill person must make a conscientious choice to take it responsibly. He or she may choose to utilize therapy and rehab. A critical choice people face is the decision to be optimistic and hopeful or to sink into dark depression.

Every illness provides us with choices. In the context of healing, the greatest choice is the decision to pursue healing! When people make that choice, they typically improve.

SMALL GROUP DISCUSSION

1. If you feel comfortable doing so, share your lists with one another. (If you prefer to maintain privacy, simply share the number of choices you had.)

2. Were you surprised by the number of choices listed? Why?

3. How did it feel to have choices during your illness? Elaborate.

4. How might it have felt if you had been denied choices? Why?

THE POWER OF CHOICES

It is vitally important to realize that you have choices to make when illness strikes. You are not left alone at the mercy of circumstances or the medical community. The truth is that you are the most important part of the process!

As we've just discussed, you will have more choices than you previously thought. It is vitally important to make your choices, because doing so is personally empowering. Making choices builds spiritual, emotional, and physical strength, which is necessary to fight illness.

When ill people are denied choices, they often suffer from depression and regression, which negatively impacts the healing process. Thus, the choices we face during illness are powerful!

A DIFFERENT KIND OF PAIN

To this point, the focus has been on making choices in regard to physical illnesses. However, *Healing Is a Choice* begins with Rachael's story. Her illness did not derive from organic causes. It was not the pain of disease. Her pain was emotional, spiritual, and psychological, and was the result of physical, sexual abuse. Rachael's pain was incessant; the pain of traumatic memories that won't go away, regardless of how hard one tries to forget.

Rachael's healing required a unique approach very different from treating the flu or setting a broken limb. She needed a treatment plan that would heal the painful emotional and psychological pain that felt so debilitating.

Sadly, healing the pain we carry in our minds is often much more challenging than taking medicine. Our physical bodies tend to respond quickly and positively to good medicines and treatments. So, when we get sick, we can take a few pills and know that, typically, we'll be better in a few days.

However, the emotional, spiritual, and psychological ills we suffer rarely respond to needles and pills. A different approach is required. The most powerful medicine for this pain includes God's Holy Spirit, pastors, counselors, trained therapists, loving families, and prayer and Scripture, just to mention a few.

So, healing is available to those battling physical ailments, and it is equally available to those battling emotional, spiritual, and psychological ailments. God cares about all forms of illness and how He can heal them.

VERY IMPORTANT

Though we acknowledge that there are many ways to be healed, *the choice* to heal, whether it is physical, spiritual, or psychological, is a personal choice each person must make. Healing is a choice!

Exercise #2: Rachael's Story

Read Rachael's story in *Healing Is a Choice*, Chapter 1, pages 1–5. If you are doing the study alone, reread the story on your own. If you are studying in a small group, ask a volunteer to read the story.

To help us understand Rachael's story more clearly, so that we might use it in a study exercise, let's outline it:

RACHAEL'S STORY

I. As a youngster, Rachael was sexually abused by an older adolescent relative.

   A. The abuse ended, but she was left with painful memories, guilt, and shame.

   B. She blamed herself and was afraid to tell anyone.

   C. She was unable to forget what happened, so she engaged in denial.

   D. When memories recurred, she pushed them deeper and deeper inside.

   E. She told herself there was no need to tell anyone.

   F. She experienced extreme and constant stomach pains.

II. After six years of silence and secrecy, Rachael shared her dark secret with a girlfriend. This was an important step for her, but she took no further steps toward healing for almost ten years.

   A. At sixteen years old, she made a brave decision to tell her mother, something she thought she'd never do.

B. Her mother pressed for more details, but Rachael could not bring herself to describe them. She pretended not to remember. (Rachael learned later that her mother questioned the whole incident, wondering if Rachael had made it up.)

C. Because Rachael seemed happy and healthy most of the time, her mother believed the abuse, if there was any, had not been damaging.

III. After high school, Rachael enrolled in a Christian college.

A. Still troubled by her past, she told her story to another good friend. It was an important healing choice for Rachael, because it connected her to someone who was able to significantly help her.

B. Her friend told Rachael she knew other people who had been abused and noted that counseling had helped them. She encouraged Rachael to seek Christian counseling.

C. At first, Rachael was reluctant. She just wanted to forget her past, but she couldn't. Her mother, who took a dim view of counseling, adopted a "don't rock the boat" attitude.

IV. Following her freshman year, Rachael found a boyfriend. For the first time, she confided in a man about her abuse. She added that she had difficulty loving herself. She was still denying her pain, and pushing the abuse into the past.

A. This time it did not work. The more she tried to push it away, the more it was on her mind. She had trouble focusing.

B. Encouraged by a close friend, Rachael made an appointment with the counselor.

C. She poured out her story, her pain, and her pent-up emotions.

D. With the help of her counselor, she gave the healing process "her best shot."

E. It was painful at times, but she made continuous progress.

V. Through it all, her boyfriend continued to be a good listener and a loyal friend.

VI. The relative who abused Rachael eventually confessed. As a result, Rachael's mom had a change of opinion and praised her daughter for her courage as she pursued counseling and healing.

Today, Rachael is deeply committed to God and appreciative to all those who poured their lives into her and supported her.

A. Rachael's healing continues, and the boyfriend who stood with her became her husband. They have been married for some time.

1. *Using a pencil or a pen, refer to the outline above and circle each opportunity Rachael had to make a healing choice. If you are studying in a small group, compare and discuss your responses.*

2. *Again, using the outline above, underline each person or event in which Rachael made the choice to connect with others. Remember,* Healing Is a Choice *teaches us that the first choice is: The important choice to connect our lives with others.*

In your small group, compare and discuss your responses.

In John 5:1–8 (NLT) we read about a man known only as "one of the men lying there . . ." at the pool of Bethesda, where the disabled people gathered. He had been an invalid for thirty-eight years. Jesus went directly to him and asked, "Would you like to get well?"

That might be one of the most important questions in Scripture. To some extent, spiritually or physically, we all must face that question. Do we want to get spiritually well? Do we want to be physically healed?

Though racked by emotional pain most of her life, Rachael pushed through it. When Rachael faced the question "Do I want to get well?" her answer was, "Yes! I want to be healed!"

So, with God's help, she began to reach out and connect to people who could help her. Rachael began to heal, because she connected with people who could facilitate her healing! Without those friends, she might still be suffering in her pain. Because of them, she is becoming the person God planned her to be!

3. *If you are doing a personal study, answer the following questions. If you are studying in a small group, discuss the questions together.*

When did Rachael realize she had a choice in her healing?

_____

Does pain ever serve a positive purpose?

_____

Why is it important to share our pain with other people?

_____

Why is it often necessary to seek professional help?

_____

What was the benefit for Rachael in confronting her abuse?

_____

How did God demonstrate His love and faithfulness to Rachael?

_____

How did Rachel's positive choices impact her healing?

_____

Could Rachael have recovered apart from the healing choices she made?

_____

GOD'S ACTION ON RACHAEL'S BEHALF

What choices did God make that led to Rachael's healing? Clearly, He was at work. For example, He provided:

- a personal sense of His presence in her life.

- courage to tell others what happened.

- friends who were caring, active listeners.

- professionals who could help her process her pain.

- redemption to help her reinterpret the abuse in her past.

- a loving husband.

- continuing healing.

GETTING THE POINT!

Isn't it wonderful to realize that God is at work in our lives in so many ways, guiding us toward the people who can help us, and moving us closer and closer to healing? Stories like Rachael's remind us:

- that people who've suffered great pain can be healed.

- that God is faithful.

- that we need friends and loved ones who love, support, and listen.

- that the body of Christ is an important source of "connecting" when we need healing. In fact, the clearest lesson in Rachael's story is the value of connecting with others who can help us make healing choices.

So many things separate us from others. It's a long list of destructive habits, addictions, excessive work, lack of or failure in relationships, seeking fame and fortune, and more. Such things are diversions that disconnect us from what matters most: good friends and companionship. Without connection to others, we become self-centered and selfish, isolated and alone, often unaware of our own pain.

That leads us to the first big lie described in *Healing Is a Choice*.

THE FIRST BIG LIE:
"All I need to heal is just God and me!"

On the surface, this sounds great! What could be better than God and me? It's an unbeatable combination. However, rather than being truly spiritual, that statement is sanctimonious. It's a brag. All we're really doing is hiding behind God and excluding from our lives the very people He has ordained to help us. This first "big lie" boxes God in, rather than clearing a path for Him to work in us. It's false pride, and smacks of arrogance ("healing is just God and me").

In truth, this notion is a psychological ploy, a defense mechanism to keep us separated from others.

A CHRISTIAN PRINCIPLE

In Galatians 6:2, Paul issued one of the fundamental principles of Christian human relations. He said, "Share each other's troubles and problems, and in this way obey the law of Christ" (NLT).

Notice that Paul describes the mutual bearing of one another's burdens as a law! Clearly, he does not intend this to be optional. To some degree, God intends for all His children to be healing agents. We should be available to one another, and ready to respond when needed. God even puts us in communities of people precisely because we need one another so much. We are mutually indispensable! Our responsibility is to help one another in times of need.

There is an irony here. God is able to heal by Himself. However, it is instructive that He often chooses to use other people and means in the healing process. There are many ways in which He heals, and most often, they involve people. He works His healing power through His people.

"You cannot read what God has to say about connecting with each other and be convinced that He wants us to face our pain with just Him and Him alone" (page 7).

BIBLE STUDY

Take your Bible and find the Scriptures listed below. These verses make the strong point that God's preferred way for us to live is in community with one another, connected, and functioning as agents of healing and grace. After each reference, summarize in your own words what the verse says about being connected with one another.

1. *Romans 12:5*

_____

_____

_____

_____

2. *Romans 12:15*

_____

_____

_____

_____

3. *Romans 15:14*

_____

_____

_____

_____

4. *1 Corinthians 12:25*

_____

_____

_____

_____

5. *1 Thessalonians 5:11*

_____

_____

_____

_____

6. *Ephesians 5:21*

_____

_____

_____

_____

7. *Ephesians 4:2*

_____

_____

_____

_____

8. Hebrews 10:24

_____

_____

_____

_____

9. 1 Peter 4:10

_____

_____

_____

_____

10. James 5:16

_____

_____

_____

_____

11. Galatians 6:2

_____

_____

_____

_____

HAMILTON'S EXAMPLE

Read again the story of Hamilton on pages 9 and 10. His is a great example of how isolation and secrecy work against our mental health. Hamilton's healing came when he stopped disconnecting and starting reinvesting with people.

The reason the choice to connect is the first choice is that God needs people in your life to bring about the benefits of the other choices. The other choices do no good for the hermit. You need others, and the alienation you experience in your pain blocks them off from you. So you must take a step away from your comfortable surroundings and allow others to minister to you and nurture you—no matter how difficult it is. (*Healing Is a Choice*, page 11)

Like Hamilton and thousands of other people, independence seems to be the great goal of life. It's "macho" to say, "I don't need anyone else," "I am a self-made person," and "I will handle whatever comes my way." Some people might say that "all I need is just God and me," but what they really mean is, "I'll do fine by myself, and God can just watch over my shoulder."

Such cultural pride and arrogance doom us to relational failures, because we simply were not created to be that isolated. Besides, such an independent attitude is an illusion. It is not real.

IS THERE A DOWNSIDE TO CONNECTEDNESS?

Just as the pride mentioned in the previous paragraphs sabotages our relationships with God and others, there are some risks in connecting to other people. People may be inexperienced in building relationships. Perhaps they've never had a close friend and don't know where to begin.

Your parents may not have known how to connect with others. Therefore, you are left without a model to follow. Or, you might have made a meaningful connection with someone only to be betrayed or abandoned.

Perhaps you connected with someone who "smothers" you, stealing your autonomy and individuality. You may have befriended someone whose real goal is to dominate and control you.

There are risks involved in any relationship. Still, the value of being connected to others is positive and beneficial, justifying the risks.

Being connected in relationships is well worth the effort. We must not allow fear to keep us isolated and alone. God does not intend us to live that way.

Furthermore, as *Healing Is a Choice* makes clear, we often have to make connections with others despite our pain or disappointment. We were created to live, grow, and prosper in interrelated, mutually dependent, godly communities.

JESUS SHOWED US HOW TO CONNECT

Jesus was one of the most connected people who ever lived! He developed His own support group, with whom He shared life for the better part of three years. Though crowds sometimes wore Him out, He still attended to the people; teaching, healing, even feeding them. He ignored societal boundaries that excluded women, children, lepers, and Gentiles. In fact, Jesus went out of His way to connect with such folks! He embraced everyone, even the most sanctimonious and legalistic in society. He saved the life of a woman caught in adultery. He restored the warped mind of a demoniac. He wept at the death of a loved one. He shared meals with tax collectors. He moved easily among His peers. Jesus connected without fear or reservation. He took the risks of reaching out and building relationships.

In the end, He was even betrayed by one with whom He had significantly connected. Still, it did not deter Him. He responded by dying for the entire human race, connecting us all by means of the Cross.

If we ever needed an example of how to connect with others, it is Jesus. We may never replicate what He did, but we can try to be more like Him, especially in regard to connecting with people.

Journaling

Take a few minutes and think about chapter 1. Review it in your mind, or go back and skim the pages. Use the questions and spaces below to guide your journaling.

How do you connect with others?

_____

_____

_____

Have you been successful, or is it hard for you?

_____

_____

_____

Which parts of chapter 1 spoke most clearly to you?

_____

_____

_____

Did you see yourself in any of the examples mentioned in chapter 1?

_____

_____

_____

Did you have good role models to show you how to connect?

_____

_____

_____

Do you carry pain inside that you need to release? With whom might you do that?

_____

_____

_____

One of the best places to connect with others is a Christian church. Are you invested in a church? If not, how could you move toward connecting with a congregation?

_____

_____

_____

Have you experienced healing of any kind as a result of connecting with others?

_____

_____

_____

Can you give up your pain and allow God's healing power to work in your life, regardless of how He may choose to express it?

_____

_____

_____

Prayerful Meditation

Find a quiet, relaxing place where you are comfortable and uninterrupted. Take a few minutes and meditate on the information in chapter 1. Sit quietly and clear your mind of the day's events. Think about the goodness and greatness of God. Slow down your thoughts and focus on Christ. Ask the Holy Spirit to speak to your mind. Be patient. Listen quietly and wait for the Spirit to speak.

The Holy Spirit may want to encourage you to be bolder and more confident as you connect with others. He may want to challenge you to take the risk of being healed of past hurts. He may want you to roll your cares into His hands. Do you want to be healed? Jesus is able to do it.

Prayer

Heavenly Father, thank You for the encouragement I received from this chapter. Help me to examine my heart and mind, and to identify the pain I may feel. From the power of Your Spirit, give me the courage to move toward connectedness with others, and ultimately, healing. Increase my confidence in You. Where I am weak and hesitant to act, give me strength. Increase my faith. Open my heart to others, and give me a willingness to invest in Your people, the community of faith. I give You my life; mind, soul, and spirit. Through Jesus Christ, my Savior and friend. Amen.

2

THE SECOND CHOICE:
The Choice to Feel Your Life

THE SECOND BIG LIE:
*"Real Christians should have a real peace
in all circumstances."*

IMAGINE WHAT MIGHT HAPPEN IF WE FELT NO PAIN. WE MIGHT say, "No pain? That would be great!" But the opposite is true. The absence of pain would create unimaginable problems. We might suffer serious physical illnesses and not be aware, because there would be no pain to warn us.

What could happen if there were no nerves in your feet, so that you could not feel anything as you walked about? Suppose you were running barefoot through the woods and stepped on several sharp pieces of a broken bottle. Your feet might suffer severe cuts with profuse bleeding. You might lapse into shock or even bleed to death, because there was no pain to warn you.

What if your appendix became infected, threatening to burst? Without pain to let you know something serious was happening, you might die from toxemia.

Ashlyn Blocker is a small child who was born with an ailment that prevents her from feeling pain. As a result, she is often in danger of hurting herself. Her food must be cooled, and ice cubes are dropped into her soup so she won't burn herself. Her mother said, "I'd give anything for her to feel pain."

How ironic! Most of us hate pain. We view it as something to be avoided. It hurts. The bottom line is that we view pain as bad. Given the choice, human beings move as quickly as possible from pain to pleasure. Yet, Ashlyn's mom desperately wishes her child could feel pain!

The truth is that pain can be very helpful. How often have you gone to your doctor or taken a sick child to the clinic, and the attending physician asks, "Where does it hurt?" Pain gives the doctor direction as she looks for the source of illness. Pain is not the enemy.

THE SECOND CHOICE:
The Choice to Feel Your Life

Key Scripture: *Your promise revives me; it comforts me in all my troubles.*

—Psalm 119:50 NLT

The powerful truth is, "when we feel our lives, we are tuned in to pain as it emerges and can resolve it before our lives begin to revolve around it."

Pain can be all-consuming. It demands our total attention. It's hard to deny or push aside. Culturally, we seem dedicated to doing everything possible to eradicate pain. Billions of dollars are spent to prevent or alleviate it. The unwritten goal seems to be do anything possible, at any cost, to avoid the feeling of pain.

However, whether we deny it or medicate it, there is no guarantee it will go away. It is there for a purpose. Until we've acknowledged and addressed the cause of our pain, we will continue to suffer its misery.

The psalmist experienced considerable pain in his life. He learned an important principle that we all should affirm: We are comforted in our pain by the truth that God preserves our lives (Ps. 119:50).

An Important Principle

In the book we read, "What is true of physical pain and the body is true for emotional pain and the soul." Pain can be physical, but it can also be emotional, psychological, and spiritual. In fact, emotional pain is often much worse than its physical counterpart. It can take root in our psyches and embark on a deadly mission to wound our hearts.

Typically, medications and treatments heal physical pain, but the pain we bear in our hearts and minds does not respond well to organic medicines.

Chapter 2 describes the challenge of dealing with emotional pain, as illustrated in Laurie's story.

Exercise #1
Read Laurie's story again (pages 28–32). If you are studying in a small group, ask a volunteer to read it aloud.

Respond to the following questions in the spaces provided. If you are studying in a small group, discuss your answers together.

1. *What was the source of Laurie's pain?*

_____

_____

2. *Laurie's husband confessed his affair, repented, sought forgiveness, and recommitted to their marriage. However, as he improved, Laurie seemed to get worse. What happened to Laurie?*

_____

_____

3. *What caused Laurie's pain to intensify, even as her husband recovered and was restored?*

_____

_____

4. *What did Laurie desperately need to do?*

_____

_____

LAURIE'S STRUGGLE WITH HER PAIN

Laurie's story is filled with irony. At a time when she thought all was well with her life, her husband's life was a disaster. When Laurie discovered his affair and confronted him, he did all the right things. He confessed, repented, apologized, and changed. As a result he felt better, cleansed and restored. People were amazed as they noted the positive changes in his life. In a weird way, he became a local hero. Bad guy makes good! He was the center of attention. Everyone assumed that Laurie felt great, too; but she didn't! On the contrary, the better her husband did, the worse she felt. Why?

Laurie never had an opportunity to acknowledge and deal with her personal pain.

She needed to grieve, to be angry and process through the painful emotions caused by her husband's infidelity.

People failed to acknowledge her personal pain. Strangely, they encouraged her to deny it. So, Laurie languished. She had done nothing wrong. She hadn't engaged in an affair. She had been faithful and committed, yet she was the one racked by pain.

The one thing Laurie desperately needed was to acknowledge and feel the pain that lay suppressed inside her. It made her miserable! Holding her pain inside, she shut down emotionally, stopped connecting with others, and sank into depression.

CONNECTING AND FEELING

At this point, one of the great values of *Healing Is a Choice* emerges. Remember that chapter 1 encouraged readers to reach out and connect with others who could help them heal. This chapter encourages readers to feel their pain. Yet, finding the courage and commitment to experience pain often depends on those with whom we have connected.

We need to experience our pain rather than deny it. But we also need a safe environment in which to do it. That "safe environment" is our circle of loving, caring friends. We need those who will encourage us to feel, and stay near us while we do. We need friends who will not be afraid when our emotions are uncontrollable, and who will remain until they subside.

It is practically impossible to feel and express one's pain without the support of those who love you and can provide a safe environment for your feelings.

Laurie was missing one important connection that trapped her in unresolved pain. Her husband was a changed man, for the better. He received great applause and praise for his reformation. He had done everything right, *except address his wife's pain.* Laurie's missing connection was her husband! Laurie was left to languish in pain. Her husband needed to connect with her feelings, and to acknowledge his role in causing them. "He needed to show her in a profound way that he was willing to pay a price for what he had done" (*Healing Is a Choice*, p. 35). Such an act of connection might have dramatically speeded Laurie's recovery.

EMOTIONS AND FEELINGS

This chapter focuses on the importance of facing and experiencing our emotions.

The American Heritage Dictionary defines *emotion* as "a mental state that arises spontaneously rather than through conscious effort and is often accompanied by physiological changes; a feeling."[1] Emotions are instinctive, innate patterns of behaviors. They come with us at birth. Emotions are the "part of the consciousness that involves feeling."

The word "emotion" comes from a Latin word meaning "to move." Perhaps that is why we often refer to our emotions as "moving us" to tears, joy, excitement, etc.

Emotions come in a wide variety. Some are sad. Some are joyous. Some are frightening. People are very comfortable with some of their emotions, but can become quite upset by others. Let's do a personal appraisal of feelings.

Exercise #2: Feelings Appraisal

Read through the list of emotions below, one at a time. After each word, describe your reaction(s) to the feeling listed on the line provided.

Example: Hope—Makes me feel upbeat. Inspires optimism.

Emotions	Reactions
Anger	
Despair	
Fear	
Hate	
Hope	
Love	
Sadness	
Joy	
Grief	
Guilt	
Worry	

Answer the following questions:

If you are studying in a small group, use the following questions for discussion.

1. *Which emotions would you describe as negative?*

_____

_____

_____

_____

2. *Which emotions would you describe as positive?*

_____

_____

_____

_____

3. *Which emotions would you describe as most destructive?*

_____

_____

_____

_____

4. *Which emotions would you describe as most constructive?*

_____

_____

_____

_____

PERSONAL REFLECTION

Take some time to analyze your responses. If you journal, you might consider using these questions in that process.

1. Which emotions do you experience most often?

2. Are the emotions you feel most often positive or negative?

3. Do you find that some emotions seem to be constantly present in your life? For example, do you feel sad most of the time? Fearful? Angry? Hopeful?

Far too many people try "to bury their emotions because they were often told that to feel them would be wrong." Can you remember a parent or relative saying, "Don't feel sad," "You shouldn't be so angry," or "You're just a worrywart!"

Though it might be unintentional, such language is an effort to deny your feelings. Most likely, your parents or friends were uncomfortable with those feelings, or felt it was inappropriate to express them. How sad! When people are denied their feelings, they get stuck in them. They feel isolated, disconnected, and emotionally paralyzed.

There is no easy way through emotional and spiritual pain. It cannot be denied, buried, or ignored. We can't magically erase it as we do the writing on a chalkboard. If we don't look our pain in the eye, experience it and process it, it can "store up" in us, and we become consumed with the effort to find something to relieve our pain.

To make matters worse, many people suffering from intense emotional pain try to self-medicate using drugs, food, alcohol, money, sex, gambling, reckless risk-taking and more. Sadly, these things never work, and they always compound the problem. It's like trying to cure lung cancer with an aspirin. Thus, pain increases.

Denying our feelings is a debilitating effort. It's much better to experience the pain and learn how to express it appropriately.

Rather than suppress feelings, we need to pay careful attention to them, because they are barometers of our mental health.

What people need most is a genuine cure, the kind that only comes from God's Holy Spirit and the connection of loving, caring friends.

Exercise #3: Bible Study

Jesus experienced a wide range of feelings, from anger to weeping to joy. He did not deny His feelings, but felt free to feel and express His emotions. Jesus acknowledged His feelings. He

- wept (John 11:35).

- was compassionate (Mark 1:41).

- loved people, and had deep personal affection for friends (John 11:3).

- was tired and worn out (John 4:6).

- laughed and played with children (Mark 10:16).

- was so angry with corrupt temple officials that He overturned their tables (Matt. 21:12).

Read the Scriptures listed below. Each one describes something about the pain and sorrow Jesus experienced. After each Scripture reference, describe in your own words what the verse means, and how it describes Jesus' experience of physical and emotional pain.

1. *Isaiah 53:3–9*

_____

_____

_____

2. Matthew 26 (the entire chapter, but especially vv. 38–40, 42)

_____

_____

_____

3. Matthew 27:46

_____

_____

_____

One thing we learn from these texts is that Jesus knows what pain is like, because He experienced it personally. He is acquainted with grief and sorrow. Therefore, He can empathize with us in times of suffering, and He knows the appropriate way to respond.

Remember how important it is to be connected to others during times of pain. Jesus is "a real friend [who] sticks closer than a brother" (Prov. 18:24 NLT). He has promised to stay connected to us: "I will never fail you. I will never forsake you" (Heb. 13:5 NLT). When we are connected to Him, He will be with us as we experience the deep pain in our lives.

THE VALUE OF PAIN

Pain, for all its hurts, can be a positive thing. We deny it at our own peril. The apostle Paul wrote,

> We can rejoice, too, when we run into problems and trials, for we know that they are good for us—they help us learn to endure. And endurance develops strength of character in us,

and character strengthens our confident expectation of salvation. And this expectation will not disappoint us. For we know how dearly God loves us, because he has given us the Holy Spirit to fill our hearts with his love. (Rom. 5:3–5 NLT)

Consider the positive impact of pain. It gets our attention. Break a finger, stub a toe, suffer a migraine headache, or experience the rejection of a close friend, and you will pay attention!

Pain is a great motivator. When we experience it, we are moved to action. Our full attention will focus on getting medicine, reconciling a broken relationship, or doing whatever is necessary to get relief.

Pain gives us direction. If we are enduring a high fever, have lost a job, or experienced a divorce, pain moves us toward healing, spurs us to find employment, and pushes us to make a fresh start.

Pain prompts us to connect with others. It is true that some folks, when enduring great pain, turn inward and isolate themselves. What they need most are good friends who can reach out to them. However, most people seek the support of others from whom they can draw strength as they walk through the valley of pain.

Whether it is a physician, a health practitioner, a counselor, or a trusted friend, the need to connect during the "pain-to-healing" process is profound. A physician has the expertise to diagnose and prescribe medicine. A counselor can help us examine the emotional pain we endure and guide us toward the means of dealing with it. A friend stands solidly with us in our pain; supporting, praying, helping, and caring.

Pain may not feel good, but it is not always our enemy. It has the power to spur us on to emotional and spiritual growth.

THE SECOND BIG LIE:

"Real Christians should have a real peace in all circumstances."

There are some religious groups who teach that "true" faith means we will never be ill, experience failure, have financial problems, suffer marital trauma, or have to endure pain or suffering.

In order to prove themselves faithful and live up to such impossible expectations, they have to engage in denial. They often construct a world-view that allows them to endure all manner of problems, while they magically "confess" just the opposite. They experience intense emotional pain, but confess that all is well.

The notion that real Christians can move through life with uninterrupted peace is psychological denial written as theology.

In the real world, all people are subject to the human condition. We all experience pain, illness, trouble, fatigue, grief, and anger, just as Jesus did. We experience the full range of human emotions, good and bad. It's important that we understand this, so we don't feel compelled to hide our pain behind a facade.

We should acknowledge the difference between objective peace and subjective peace. Objective peace occurs in a religious context. It is the peace that we have because Jesus Christ died for us and, as a result, there is no enmity between God and us. We have the peace of God that passes understanding. It is a spiritual fact, and does not waver, even though we may have all sorts of human experiences, good and bad (Phil. 4:7).

Subjective peace is what we have been discussing. It relies heavily on human emotions. We feel settled, happy, and peaceful. Life is relatively calm. Our worries are few, our bills are paid, our relationships are healthy, and life's existential pressures have diminished. It feels great, but we know that, in a moment's time, subjective peace could be shattered. A car accident, financial failure, trouble with a child, losing a job, or experiencing a heated argument with a spouse can all disturb one's peace, and for quite a while.

Real Christians can have objective peace with God at all times, but no human being will experience subjective peace all the time. As mentioned above, all people are subject to the human condition.

Here is a very important fact: The quality of our mental health may depend on recognizing the important distinction between objective and subjective peace.

Exercise #4: Bible Study (2 Cor. 4:7–10, 16, 17) The Bible consistently makes the point that we experience both the joys and pains of life. No one is exempted.

By listing the statements in 2 Corinthians 4:7–10, 16, 17 under "Bad News" and "Good News" categories, we get a vivid picture of the contrasting nature of real life. In this paradigm, we see that life is about limitations, pain, and fragileness.

> But this precious treasure—this light and power that now shine within us—is held in perishable containers, that is, in our weak bodies.

At the same time, it is about hope, recovery, and victory.

> . . . we are not crushed and broken.

Read through the list and note that we experience normal human challenges (Bad News), but also the grace and care of God (Good News).

Bad News	**Good News**
2 Corinthians 4:7	
But this precious treasure—this light and power that now shine within us—is held in perishable containers, that is, our weak bodies [we are fragile creatures],	so everyone can see that our glorious power is from God and is not our own.
2 Corinthians 4:8	
We are pressed on every side by troubles [life is filled with pressure],	but we are not crushed and broken.
We are perplexed,	but we don't give up and quit.
2 Corinthians 4:9	
We are hunted down,	but God never abandons us.
We get knocked down,	but we get up again and keep going.
2 Corinthians 4:10	
Through suffering, these bodies of ours constantly share in the death of Jesus	so that the life of Jesus may also be seen in our bodies.
2 Corinthians 4:12	
So we live in the face of death,	but it has resulted in eternal life for you.
2 Corinthians 4:16	
Though our bodies are dying,	our spirits are being renewed every day. That is why we never give up.
2 Corinthians 4:17	
For our present troubles are quite small and won't last very long,	yet they produce for us an immeasurably great glory that will last forever!

This way of looking at 2 Corinthians 4 helps us understand that the normal Christian life is impacted by good and bad, highs and lows, victories and challenges. This is real life, and it is very important for us to experience—to feel—all of it. At times it may seem frightening. Life can be very tough. But regardless of the circumstances, God is faithful and His Holy Spirit is always close to us, ready to help in our time of need.

A Pain Inventory and Feelings Checkup

The book suggests taking a pain inventory and feelings checkup (*Healing Is a Choice*, pp. 44–46), so let's do that.

INSTRUCTIONS:

1. *Select a quiet place away from noise, crowds, and busyness.*

2. *Be still and try to quiet your mind so that you can focus without interruption. In this exercise, you may find answers to questions you did not even know you were avoiding. You may find some areas that are sensitive and need resolution. Or, you may discover that feeling your life is not something to avoid.*

3. *Ask yourself these questions:*

What am I afraid of?

_____

_____

What is missing?

Am I empty?

What am I filling up on?

Why am I refusing to feel?

What feelings am I avoiding?

Look at your responses. Do you see a pattern? Do you seem to be hiding from your pain? Are you failing to connect with others? Continue by answering the next set of questions dealing with fear:

Am I afraid of rejection?

Am I afraid of being inadequate?

_____

_____

Am I afraid someone might come to control me?

_____

_____

Do I avoid doing things because I am afraid of failing?

_____

_____

Am I afraid of doing nothing significant during my life?

_____

_____

If you answered yes to any of these questions, take some time and consider why you are experiencing the pain of fear. Analyze the question(s) until you can answer no to the questions. Next, answer the five questions below that deal with anger:

Do I hold a grudge?

_____

_____

Am I angry because I feel controlled?

_____

_____

Is my past in my present because of anger toward someone who hurt me?

_____

_____

Am I seeking revenge in any form?

_____

_____

Does my anger lead me to negative statements about anyone?

_____

_____

If you answered yes to any of these questions, take some time and consider why you are experiencing the pain of anger. Analyze the questions(s) until you can answer no to the questions. Finally, answer the five questions below dealing with guilt and shame:

Am I feeling guilty about a current habit?

_____

_____

Do I experience shame from something someone did to me?

_____

_____

Am I knowingly involved in a sin?

_____

_____

When I feel guilty, am I shutting my guilt down with food or drink?

Is there anything I could change to reduce the guilt?

If you answered yes to any of these questions, take some time and consider why you are feeling shame and guilt. Think about the question(s) until you can answer no to the questions.

THE PASSION OF CHRIST

In 2004, Mel Gibson created a stir throughout the world by releasing a movie titled *The Passion of the Christ*. In the most graphic version of the death of Christ ever produced, the movie confronted viewers with the brutal reality of Jesus' physical abuse and ultimate death. The movie was very nearly too painful to watch.

What is clearly conveyed is that Jesus chose to "feel" His pain. He did not run away from it or deny it. He felt it all. And, the most scandalous thing is that He experienced the pain for us. He created a means by which we can deal with our pain, be it spiritual, emotional, or physical.

Thanks to Jesus, we no longer have a need to deny or suppress our pain. We can feel it and overcome it, and roll it over onto Him, because He knows how it feels and never leaves or forsakes us (1 Pet. 5:7).

JOURNALING

Take a few minutes and think about chapter 2. Review it in your mind, or go back and scan the pages. Use the questions and spaces below to guide your journaling.

Why do we fear pain?

_____

_____

_____

Has pain ever had a positive impact on your life?

_____

_____

_____

What parts of chapter 2 spoke most clearly to you?

_____

_____

_____

Were you able to personally identify with aspects of chapter 2?

_____

_____

_____

How have you handled pain in your life?

_____

_____

_____

Do you acknowledge and feel your pain, or do you deny or suppress it?

_____

_____

_____

Does God use pain to shape our character?

_____

_____

_____

Have you ever experienced the consequences of denied pain?

_____

_____

_____

What pain might you be holding on to at this time in your life?

_____

_____

_____

How can you let go of that pain?

_____

_____

_____

PRAYERFUL MEDITATION

Find a quiet, relaxing place where you are comfortable and uninterrupted. Take a few minutes and meditate on the information in chapter 2. Sit quietly for a few minutes. Listen to your heartbeat and appreciate that you are alive and can feel.

Clear your mind and focus on Jesus Christ. Quietly sing or hum a favorite hymn. Think about the goodness and greatness of God. Ask the Holy Spirit to clear the clutter and busyness from your mind. Be patient. Listen quietly and wait for the Spirit to speak to your mind.

The Holy Spirit may want to encourage you to be braver when it comes to feeling your pain. He may want to challenge you to take the risk of acknowledging your pain.

Experience the presence of Christ, who will gladly take your pain and help you bear it.

PRAYER

Heavenly Father, hear my honest prayer and my sincere concerns. At times I am overcome with pain. People I love are hurting and I don't know how to help. My health is failing and I can't stop it. The quality of my work is slipping and I am afraid I won't be able to keep up. I feel distant from You. Sometimes I think I have more pain than joy. Is that the way it's supposed to be? I need help. I need Your help. Thank You for the challenge and encouragement I have received from this chapter. Help me to acknowledge my pain, feel it, and then, with Your help, move toward peace and calm. Help me examine my heart and mind honestly, and to identify the pain I carry from day to day. I acknowledge that healing my pain is a choice. From the power of Your Spirit, give me the courage to choose healing. Increase my confidence in You. Where I am weak and hesitant to act, give me strength.

Increase my faith. I give You my life; mind, soul, and spirit. Through Jesus Christ, my Savior and friend. Amen.

He will remove all of their sorrows, and there will be no more death or sorrow or crying or pain. For the old world and its evils are gone forever.

—Revelation 21:4 NLT

3

THE THIRD CHOICE:

The Choice to Investigate Your Life in Search of Truth

THE THIRD BIG LIE:

"It does no good to look back or look inside."

AUTHOR PETER GILLQUIST DESCRIBES A FOOTBALL GAME AS "20,000 people in the stadium who desperately need exercise, watching 22 people on the field who desperately need rest!" How true! Imagine that you are attending a football game. Several times during an average game, the offensive team will run a play in which a fullback, probably weighing 220 pounds or more, will get the ball and begin charging downfield toward the goal line. It's a simple play, and all teams have it in their playbooks. From the moment the fullback gets the ball, the play is utterly simple. He runs with all his might toward the goal. His blockers get in front of him to clear the path. All eleven players on the opposing team move toward the fullback and do everything in their power to tackle him, preventing him from scoring. The opposing players are all impediments to the fullback, who is trying to score. Each impediment can potentially tackle him, but if the play unfolds as planned, the blockers will remove the impediments and the fullback will score. Statistically, the defensive team is more successful than the offensive one, so the runners are most often tackled and stopped. The impediments work!

Just as the fullback faces impediments on his journey to the goal, we all face impediments as we strive for a full, healthy, productive life. Conflict is an impediment, as is the tendency to disconnect from those who can help you.

If you haven't already noticed, the theme of connecting your life with others' is sewn into each chapter of this book. Being connected to others is an important means of finding the healing we need. Disconnecting and isolating ourselves is a strategy that dooms us to failure. Typically, when a person isolates himself, he becomes his own adviser, and that usually dooms him to receive faulty advice!

We need to be connected to trusted friends, who will be honest and objective while loving and caring for us.

We move toward God because we know He loves and cares for us. We move toward family and friends, hoping for the support and love they provide. We move toward friends, who care for and support us as we deal with painful issues.

People who understand the value of connectedness move as quickly as possible to a loving, supportive group who can help them deal with troubling issues.

It is not uncommon for some people to intentionally put impediments in the road to healing. Rather than make a choice to heal, they make a choice to hinder their healing. The impediments they place in their path keep them separated from others and diminish their spiritual and emotional health.

Why do we build impediments to healing? Why would we sabotage the very things that could most help us? Why are we sometimes our own worst enemies?

The answer lies in the fact that many people go marching through life without ever dealing with their tendency to create impediments. They repeat the same mistakes and build the same roadblocks over and over. Their behavior becomes instinctive, a habit that causes continual pain.

They ignore the one thing they most need to do, which is to examine why they keep making choices that result in pain and turmoil.

We heal our lives as we begin to search for truth about why we do what we do and why we feel the way we feel.

One of the reasons premarriage counseling is so important is that it requires a couple to examine their lives prior to marriage. They must deal with past relational hurt and be sure that it is healed. When two very hurt and unaware people come together in marriage, the result is often complete and total disaster, so each person must confront their hurts and work toward healing in anticipation of marriage.

Taking unresolved conflict, unaddressed emotional pain, and unresolved issues into marriage is to fill the road ahead with impediments.

Exercise #1 Who Are Your Friends?

How do you determine the people with whom you are connected? Take a few minutes and think about your closest, most trusted friends; those who could share your deepest concerns. List their names in the spaces provided. If you have only one friend, use one line. If you need more lines, draw them in. Beneath each friend's name, describe in a couple of sentences why this person is valuable to you, how you are connected, and how being "connected" to them makes you a better person.

1. *Friend:*

_____

Why he or she is valuable to me:

_____

_____

2. *Friend:*

_____

Why he or she is valuable to me:

_____

_____

3. *Friend:*

_____

Why he or she is valuable to me:

_____

_____

4. *Friend:*

_____

Why he or she is valuable to me:

_____

_____

If you did not list anyone, you might consider your need to cultivate new friends.

Read Proverbs 18:24 in several translations (New Living Translation, King James Version, and the New International Version). Each version gives a slightly different perspective about friendship.

- The KJV encourages each of us to seek friends by reaching out and being friendly.
- The NIV encourages us to find a close friend who would be closer than a natural brother.
- The NLT says there are "friends" who destroy each other, but a real friend sticks closer than a brother.

The important point is to connect with others who will be true friends and provide support and care when needed.

THE THIRD CHOICE:
The Choice to Investigate Your Life in Search of Truth

Key Scripture: *Instead, let us test and examine our ways. Let us turn again in repentance to the* LORD.
—Lamentations 3:40 NLT

THE UNEXAMINED LIFE IS A PROBLEM!

Healing Is a Choice gives us ten important choices to make and ten lies to reject. The choice in chapter 3 is to investigate your life in search of truth.

Left to our own notions, we often lapse into self-centeredness and isolation. We often do hurtful things to ourselves and to others, then walk away shaking our heads, wondering why we do such things.

We know hurtful, angry words damage our relationships, but we utter them just the same. We desperately need to figure out why we do the things we later regret.

Chapter 3 reminds us that we heal our lives as we begin to search for truth about why we do what we do and feel the way we feel. Without introspection, we keep repeating our mistakes and sabotaging our most important relationships.

Jeremiah was most likely the writer of Lamentations. The book begins with a summary of Jerusalem's sorrows and moves quickly to Judah's hope for God's mercy.

That pattern describes most of us. We experience failure, pain, and sorrow in life. It's tough. It often depresses us and impacts our behavior. We long for relief and desperately need to recover and do life a different way.

Like Jeremiah, we look with anticipation for mercy, grace, and healing. Like ancient Israel, we have choices to make. We can languish in our sorrow, or we can make a choice to heal.

If we make the choice to heal, then we need to examine our lives in order to know where to make corrections and improvements. It is a wholesome effort to stop and take a look at life in our past, present, and where we are headed in the future.

It is very interesting that both the Old and New Testaments address the idea of self-examination. Jeremiah encourages us to "Instead, let us test and examine our ways. Let us turn again in repentance to the LORD" (Lam. 3:40 NLT).

In the New Testament, the apostle Paul challenged his readers to "examine yourselves to see if your faith is really genuine. Test yourselves. If you cannot tell that Jesus Christ is among you, it means you have failed the test" (2 Cor. 13:5 NLT).

Self-examination is a theme in both Christian spirituality and philosophy. In 399 BC, Socrates uttered the most famous quote about self-examination. In a lecture to the people, he stated that based on his persistent questioning and study of the populace, he had determined that "the unexamined life is not worth living."

That statement has become a fundamental tenet of all philosophical quests. He further explained that the citizens of Greece spent their lives pursuing material things, without asking whether they were actually important. Socrates warned that if people failed to examine their motives and actions, they would never know if they were doing the right thing. His words sound like they were meant for us.

Ironically, the unexamined life may be our own.

So many people arrive at adulthood without ever truly examining themselves. As a result, their lives are often a mess.

All of us have mysteries inside us. We don't understand why we do some things.

We are shocked by the thoughts presenting our minds. We need help to understand why we do the things we do. Consider how easily we fall into negative relational patterns.

COMMON PATTERNS IN DYSFUNCTIONAL RELATIONSHIPS

There are common patterns in human relationships. They are common and identifiable. Read again pages 50–54 in *Healing Is a Choice*. The following common relational patterns are described:

1. The overweight wife married to the sex-addicted husband.

2. A woman whose father did not provide for her or connect with her deepest needs.

3. A woman who is miserable because her father was so good. She looks to her husband to fulfill her, but he is not enough, not as good as her father.

4. A husband whose mother met his every need is angry because his wife is unwilling to do that.

5. A husband whose mother was overbearing and domineering projects all his anger toward his wife.

6. A wife is sexually rejected by her husband, who sees her as domineering like his mother. Unable to feel sexual toward his wife, he turns to pornographic images that give him a sense of control.

7. A husband and wife grow increasingly apart. Anger has melted into indifference. The husband compares his wife to pornographic images on the computer, and in his comparison, she comes up short, rejected and alienated.

Notice that these patterns are all examples of disconnection. They drive people apart rather than connect them.

Exercise #2 What Are Your Thoughts?
Use the space provided to answer the questions. If you are studying in a small group, use the questions as a discussion guide.

1. *How do relationships like those described above occur?*

_____

_____

_____

2. *How can marriages that begin with so much hope and optimism fall into such turmoil, conflict, and disappointment?*

_____

_____

_____

3. *Why is it so hard for people to become involved in the self-examination that might heal their lives?*

_____

_____

_____

The answers to these questions reside in the minds and hearts of the two people involved. They brought themselves to the marriage, with all their "baggage" from the past.

We need to carefully consider the "why" behind our actions and feelings. Why do we do what we do? What is motivating us?

MYSTERIES OF THE MIND

Humans are complex, mysterious creatures. We can function in a relatively normal way. We can maintain relationships with a modicum of affection and commitment. We can tolerate huge amounts of relational pain.

On the other hand, we can make lifelong commitments to other people. We are capable of incredible acts of self-sacrifice and compassion.

Throw into that mix the fact we are capable of doing strange and unexpected things with no plausible explanation. The mysteries in our minds can damage the most important relationships we have.

But there is good news! Healing is a choice, and we are capable of making healing choices. Healing these mysteries requires us to look into our past and present and future and consider "why" we do what we do. We must identify the defective patterns in our relationships and correct them. Such work turns mysteries into knowledge and gives us hope.

THE THIRD BIG LIE:
"It does no good to look back or look inside."

As you begin to examine your life, there are plenty of people who will say, "Forget that! The past is behind us. You don't gain anything by looking back." It is possible for someone to be "stuck" in the past. Something so traumatic happened to a person in the past that he was left with unresolved issues. They are burdened by the residue of the past: guilt, shame, remorse, anger, anxiety, fear, mistrust, and more. Thus, they cannot move forward. These people dwell in the past. By definition, *dwell* means to "live" or "reside." Thus, they spend their entire lives "dwelling" in the past. However, there is a huge difference between introspection and "living in the past." Introspection allows us to look at our past, learn from it, and then move into the future with new strength. The old cliché "We learn from our mistakes" works only if we pause to look back and examine them. It is a wholesome, productive effort from which most people benefit greatly.

Scripture encourages us to forget "the past and [look] forward to what lies ahead" (Phil. 3:13 NLT). The point is that we should have a future orientation.

The big lie suggests that there is nothing to be gained by looking back or looking inward. In fact, just the opposite is true. Our mistakes tell us where we don't want to go again. If we accept the big lie, we are forever doomed in our past.

Encountering the Truth About You

It is important that we discover the truth about ourselves. That might be one reason why you are reading this book. You sense you are not whole. You wish you could change the destructive patterns of your life. Are you willing to examine yourself?

The truth is that you may need help. Most of us are reluctant to identify our own weaknesses and problems. We're not sure how to deal with them. We fear they may intensify if we expose them. We are afraid people will reject us if they find out what we're really like. However, as we mentioned earlier, "The unexamined life is not worth living." We will be healthier and better off if we do the hard work of examining ourselves and taking steps to change.

Taking a Searching and Fearless Moral Inventory

There is a process by which we can take a careful self-examination. It requires "holding your life up to the light of truth and seeing what is there" (*Healing Is a Choice*, pp. 63–65). "It is time spent looking at your faults and defects, writing them down, and seeing what they reveal about you" (p. 63).

Instructions

There are twenty questions listed below. They will assist you as you conduct your inventory.

You do not have to share this with anyone (though it might be helpful to show a trusted, connected friend, who can provide validation through a second opinion).

Offer complete answers with plenty of information. This is not a test!

You won't be graded. You do want as complete a picture as possible.

Take as long as you like. If this work seems exhaustive or is painful, just do a few questions at a sitting.

Again, you are in control of the process, but be very honest with your responses.

QUESTIONS:

1. *Starting as early as you can remember, who were the people in your life that hurt you?*

_____

_____

_____

_____

2. *Was there anything you did to bring on that hurt, or were they solely responsible?*

_____

_____

_____

_____

3. *What was your reaction to that hurt? Did you forgive them, hold on to a grudge, or try to seek your own revenge?*

_____

_____

_____

_____

4. *Is there any way you could have altered your reaction to the hurt?*

_____

_____

_____

_____

5. *Starting as early as you can remember, who were the people in your life that you hurt?*

_____

_____

_____

_____

6. *Did they do something first that hurt you, or were you acting without provocation?*

_____

_____

_____

_____

7. *Arrange your list of those you hurt in the order of the most damage to the least.*

_____
_____
_____
_____

8. *What was your reaction when you first realized you had hurt each person?*

_____
_____
_____
_____

9. *What have you done to rectify the problem caused by your hurtful actions?*

_____
_____
_____
_____

10. *Is there anything you could do to make restitution?*

_____
_____
_____
_____

11. *Are you aware of your five greatest strengths? Write down what you think they are, and then ask five other people to tell you what they think they are.*

_____

_____

_____

_____

12. *Are you aware of your five greatest weaknesses? Write down what you think they are, and then ask five other people to tell you what they think they are.*

_____

_____

_____

_____

13. *What have you done to misuse your strengths? Have you been a good steward or have you wasted them?*

_____

_____

_____

_____

14. *What have you done to use your strengths well? Ask the same five people as in the previous questions where they have seen you use your strengths well.*

_____

_____

_____

_____

15. *What have you done to correct or work on your weaknesses?*

_____
_____
_____
_____

16. *What could you do to work on them? Make a list.*

_____
_____
_____
_____

17. *What could you do to make restitution to those you have hurt?*

_____
_____
_____
_____

18. *Who could help you walk through a path of forgiveness toward those who have hurt you?*

_____
_____
_____
_____

19. *Write down a plan to contact those you have hurt, begin contacting them if it would not cause greater damage, and take notes on the things they tell you about yourself as you discuss the past.*

_____

_____

_____

_____

20. *Ask someone to be your partner in truth. Ask that person*
    to help you discover the truth about yourself and motivate
    you to continue to work on the areas that need help.

_____

_____

_____

_____

AT LEAST ONE OTHER PERSON

On June 12, 1987, President Reagan made a speech that helped contribute to the downfall of the Soviet Union. He spoke directly to the Soviet premier and said, "Mr. Gorbachev, tear down this wall!"

That is what we need to be saying to one another. Let's tear down the walls that disconnect us from one another and have for so long confined us in our pride, shame, and anger. Walls often do more harm than good.

I am going to ask you to do something that takes great courage. Now that you've finished your twenty questions, select one person who loves you, will keep your confidence, and is committed to help you become the person God wants you to be. That person should be someone who cares for you, despite the way you sometimes are! Ask that person to give you (a) honest feedback, and (b) let them know you can handle the truth. Everyone needs one person in their life who will always love them and tell them the truth.

JOURNALING

Take a few minutes and think about chapter 3. This is an amazing chapter. It is so personal in many ways, but the fact is that we have to be personal with one another if we ever want to be authentically connected. Take some time and write about your friends and the impact they have had on your life.

PRAYERFUL MEDITATION

Consider asking a friend with whom you are very connected to join you in prayer. Find a quiet, relaxing place where you are comfortable and uninterrupted. Take a few minutes and share your thoughts from chapter 3. Share the things that left a strong impression on you. Pause and thank God for the information you gained. Point out one or two things that you think might be a challenge. Ask the Holy Spirit to empower and enable you to apply those things in your life. Sit quietly for a few minutes and listen to the Holy Spirit. Feel your heartbeat and thank God for the life He has given you. Ask how you can commit your life in service to Jesus Christ.

Think about the love and faithfulness of God. Ask the Holy Spirit to speak to you about your life. Be patient. Listen quietly and wait for the Spirit to move. Ask the Spirit to help you evaluate your life to be sure you are walking in faith. Ask the Lord to provide you with good friends with whom you can grow spiritually. "Give all your worries and cares to God, for he cares about what happens to you" (1 Pet. 5:7 NLT).

PRAYER

Heavenly Father, hear my honest prayer and my sincere concerns. At times I feel trapped by my past. I've had overwhelming pain, and even some guilt and shame. I don't always know how to interpret the events of my life, or reinterpret them. There are some things in my life I simply cannot change. Thank You for the challenge and encouragement I have received from this chapter. Help me to acknowledge my pain and then, with Your help, move toward peace and calm. Help me examine my heart and mind honestly, and to identify the pain I carry from day to day. I acknowledge that healing my pain is a choice. From the power of Your Spirit, give me the courage to choose healing. Increase my confidence in You. Where I am weak and hesitant to act, give me strength. Increase my faith. I give You my life; mind, soul, and spirit. Through Jesus Christ, my Healer. Amen.

REJOICE AND SING!

If you know this chorus, sing it to conclude your devotion. If you don't know it, select a song or hymn of your choice.

THE STEADFAST LOVE OF THE LORD

The steadfast love of the Lord never ceases.
His mercies never come to an end.
They are new every morning, new every morning.
Great is Thy faithfulness, O Lord.
Great is Thy faithfulness.

4

THE FOURTH CHOICE:
The Choice to Heal Your Future

THE FOURTH BIG LIE:
"Time heals all wounds."

THE MAN OF LA MANCHA IS A MORALISTIC TALE ABOUT A fictional character, Don Quixote. The story is delightful and filled with Christian themes. In 1972, Joe Darion wrote a song, "The Impossible Dream," for a stage production of the story. Mitch Leigh wrote the music, and the song is now widely known and performed throughout the world. Read the words:

"THE IMPOSSIBLE DREAM"

To dream the impossible dream,
To fight the unbeatable foe
To bear with unbearable sorrow
To run where the brave dare not go
To right the unrightable wrong
To love pure and chaste from afar
To try when your arms are too weary
To reach the unreachable star

This is my quest

To follow that star

No matter how hopeless

No matter how far

To fight for the right

Without question or pause

To be willing to march into hell

For a heavenly cause

And I know if I'll only be true

To this glorious quest

That my heart will lie peaceful and calm

When I'm laid to my rest

And the world will be better for this

That one man, scorned and covered with scars

Still strove with his last ounce of courage

To reach the unreachable star.

Darion's song has Quixote describing his dream to do something great with his life. Listen to some of his dreams: "fight the unbeatable foe," "right unrightable wrongs," "live pure and chaste," "fight for the right," "be willing to march into hell for a heavenly cause," and "die in peace."

Quixote was a dreamer. His dreams were noble and righteous. They guided his life and inspired his quest.

What kind of dreams did you have early in life? You might have dreamed of being a great orator or a professional athlete. Perhaps you imagined being a talented musician, a teacher, or having a happy family. Did you set your sights on becoming an entrepreneur, creating businesses of your own? Have you dreamed of doing something great for the people of the world by giving your life in service to the poor, sick, or imprisoned?

Sometimes other people have dreams for you. Your parents may have told you that you'd grow up someday to be a minister or a doctor. They might have told you that you could be anything you wanted to be, so go for it! For most people in this generation, the dream of our parents is that we will do better than they did. They have extraordinary high expectations for us.

What kind of dreams do you have today? Maybe you've faced the fact that some of your early dreams will never become real. You've discovered that you can't throw a 90 mile-an-hour fastball across the inside corner of the plate! You're not comfortable speaking in front of crowds. Academia is not where your interest lies. The "9 to 5" business day is not your style.

There is nothing wrong with having great dreams, as long as we don't hold them too tightly. A dream is just that. It is an imagined future, not a reality. Many of our dreams never materialize. If we hold too tightly to them, we set ourselves up for hurt, disappointment, and failure. We may become despondent about our future, fearful that our lives will have no significance. Our dreams become losses.

Some people have their dreams stolen from them. They spend their entire lives grieving its loss. Still others grieve the loss of a childhood stolen from them by a molester, or a disease, or a disability. Life is filled with losses. Our challenge is to acknowledge our losses, grieve them, and then move on as best we can into the future.

THE FOURTH CHOICE:
The Choice to Heal Your Future

Key Scripture: *So don't worry about tomorrow, for tomorrow will bring its own worries. Today's trouble is enough for today.*
—Matthew 6:34 NLT

DRAGGING THE PAST INTO THE FUTURE

Some people are very different from those mentioned in the introduction. They never had an opportunity to create dreams. As children, they were demoralized and told "you'll never amount to anything," and "you're no good!" Their spirits were broken early in life, and they lost the capacity to have hope for the future. Their past is filled with emotional scars that are not yet healed.

Some people had dreams they let slip away.

1. *Read again the story in* Healing Is a Choice, *pp. 71–73. To experience deep love, and then lose it is an incredible loss. If we believe that the loss is a result of our own behavior, the pain we feel is compounded with guilt. Often, it is simply too great to reveal, so we hold it inside, hidden from the world. We experience emotional pain that is just as intense as physical pain. We need to diagnose it, treat it, and let it heal, so that our future will be healthy.*

2. *Take a moment and answer this question: What are some of the deep losses you have experienced that continue to cause you emotional pain? If you are studying in a small group of connected friends, you might want to discuss this together. However, be sure everyone is comfortable with public discussion.*

_____

_____

_____

_____

_____

Here is an important truth. We each must make a healing choice to grieve our losses and let them go.

William Shakespeare wrote, "What is past is prologue."[1] By that he meant that it is possible for us to continually reintroduce our past into our future.

We cannot take past hurts and losses with us into the future without painful consequences. We have to accept life as it is. Doing that, we heal our future by removing from it the constant pain of our past. Thus, the future is less encumbered. We are free to look ahead without regret. We recover hope, because we make a choice to heal the pain of the past.

The events in our past are tied to memory, and we are born with good memories, so releasing past hurts can be a challenge. These are necessary losses. *Healing Is a Choice* makes the point dramatically on page 74: "When we resist grieving (our losses), we drag our pain with us all through our lives."

Exercise #1: Thinking About Grieving
Who thinks of grieving as a good thing? Normally, it's extraordinarily sad.

However, appropriate grieving can be one of the most healing events in life.

1. *Read Karen's story on pp. 74–76 again. Answer and discuss the following questions. If you are studying in a small group, discuss your answers together.*

(a) Why did Karen's father reject her?

_____

_____

_____

_____

(b) How often did Karen's father reject her?

_____

_____

_____

_____

(c) Is it likely he did this more often than Karen's story recounts?

_____

_____

_____

_____

(d) How must Karen have felt throughout life, having never received affection from her father?

_____

_____

_____

_____

(e) How did you feel when the story noted that Karen's father never called her by name?

_____
_____
_____
_____

*(f) How do you react to Karen's repeated attempts to get
her father to acknowledge and meet with her?*

_____
_____
_____
_____

*(g) Karen never grieved the loss of her dad. As a result, she
could not move toward the future without her dad
casting a long shadow over it. She had to take him out
of her future. How did she do that?*

_____
_____
_____
_____

Healing Is a Choice describes the important decision Karen made.
"She could accept reality, grieve the loss, and let go of the expectation; or she could spend her life feeling the pain as if it were yester-
day. Grieving allows you to move on, free of the pain and agony."

She could not change or control her father. The awful reality of
his rejection would always be there, but Karen's choice to heal
ensured that it would not interfere with her life any longer. She chose
to leave the past behind and move courageously into her future.

JESUS AND GRIEF

We should be very thankful that Jesus came to us in human form, so He could identify with us in every aspect of our lives. What would we do if Jesus could not identify with out grief? It's such a painful and debilitating emotion! How would we be able to bear it?

Not only did Jesus understand grief, but He was well acquainted with it. "He was despised and rejected—a man of sorrows, acquainted with bitterest grief" (Isa. 53:3 NLT).

It makes us wonder how much grief He witnessed during His earthly ministry, and how much He attended to. It was, no doubt, more than we can imagine. Some of His responses to grief must surely be assumed in the passage that says, "And I suppose that if all the other things Jesus did were written down, the whole world could not contain the books" (John 21:25 NLT).

We are comforted by the fact that Jesus understands our losses and our grief. He is familiar with the attending emotions and struggles. He is guiding us toward a better future. However, we must cooperate with Him and accept His help.

From a biblical perspective, God always has something to say about our lives and, specifically, our future. The words He spoke to Jeremiah have relevance for every believer: "'For I know the plans I have for you,' says the LORD. 'They are plans for good and not for disaster, to give you a future and a hope'" (Jer. 29:11 NLT).

Remember that God has plans and dreams for your future, too. As a man of sorrows and grief, He identifies with our suffering. As a man of courage, He gives us strength to face our losses. Because He wept, we can freely express our emotions. Because He has experienced life as we have, we can call on Him for help. After all, He cares deeply for us. Because He lives, we can always face tomorrow!

DEALING WITH UNGRIEVED LOSSES

On pages 77–79 of *Healing Is a Choice*, we read another story of how choices to heal impact our future. This is the story of Yvonne. Take time to read it again. Yvonne's process of grieving her losses and moving into the future gives us ten objective points to consider:

1. Explore your ungrieved losses. Try to be specific regarding the issue(s) troubling you. As a child, Yvonne was molested by someone close to her family.

2. How does the problem continue to impact your life? Yvonne realized that she remained overweight and homely at age fifty. She was not taking care of herself. She acknowledged that she used her weight as a boundary, protecting her from being used again sexually.

3. Is there collateral damage? The wall of protection Yvonne created became a barrier preventing anyone from getting too close to her. It helped her feel safe, but her isolation was part of the collateral damage inflicted on her by the molester.

4. Are you stuck in your memories? Yvonne suffered daily memories of the molestation and her parents' failure to protect her. She ultimately became obsessed over them.

5. Are your emotions failing you? Gradually, Yvonne began to feel disconnected from her emotions. She stopped crying, even in appropriate settings where crying was expected and embraced.

6. How is your anger impacting you? Yvonne began to work on her past.

7. She took the first steps in trying to forgive the molester. She began to envision him in an empty chair. She would tell him (the empty chair) how she felt, demanding that he (the empty chair) tell her why he had hurt her, and finally screaming for help. She felt deeply, but still did not cry.

8. Have you reached the core issue? For Yvonne, it was the loss of her innocence. She remembered how sweet and happy and cheerful she'd been prior to the molestation. She began to feel her losses. She began to realize how much the molester had taken from her. He had stolen her childhood and almost four decades of her adult life. She realized that her entire life was being defined by one event.

9. Have you grieved? Finally, Yvonne faced the weight of pain she had born for years. She felt emotional pain at its deepest levels: grief, sadness, and sorrow. She was able to cry again. She grieved the loss of her life. Yvonne worked hard with her counselor. She wrote and wrote in her journal. She made progress.

10. Do you sense that you are recovering? Eventually, Yvonne's grief set her free, so that she could move confidently into the future. She made one of life's greatest exchanges. She traded her grief for joy!

Perhaps you have gone through an experience similar to Yvonne's. How are you doing? Look back at the ten stages in Yvonne's journey and ask yourself, "Where am I in those stages?"

If you are struggling with letting go of grief, remember that God is on your side, loving you and assisting as you make choices to heal. He sends the Holy Spirit to minister to you in your time of trouble and pain. Consider the comfort He offers from His Word: "The LORD is good. When trouble comes, he is a strong refuge. And he knows everyone who trusts in him" (Nah. 1:7 NLT). "Give all your worries and cares to God, for he cares about what happens to you" (1 Pet. 5:7 NLT).

A DIVINE EXCHANGE

Listen to these words: "I tell you the truth, you will weep and mourn while the world rejoices. You will grieve, but your grief will turn to joy" (John 16:20 NIV). Let those words resonate in your mind. Let them take root. Take a few minutes and memorize them. "Your grief will turn to joy!" "Your grief will turn to joy!" Can it be? Really? The answer comes from the heart of God. He says, "Yes!"

When you make a healing choice to grieve, you open the door to a brighter, hopeful future. You trade pain for joy. You leave isolation and disconnection with people behind and exchange it for the joy of friendship and connectedness. You give up a way of life that doesn't work very well for a way of life that is productive. You trade an old way of living for a new way.

Exercise #2: Defenses and Pretenses

All this sounds great, and it is! However, for people who've suffered great pain most of their lives, it is important to know when they are truly working through the grief and moving ahead, rather than just digging up old hurts.

You will know you are healing as you give up "defenses" and "pretenses."

We need "defenses" to protect ourselves from more pain when we have not fully experienced grief. Sometimes this is referred to as "being defensive" or using a "defense mechanism." It's really about protecting ourselves from additional pain.

A practical example might sound like this: A dear friend notes that you seem depressed and are not physically taking care of yourself. You might respond by saying, "I feel great and there's nothing wrong with the way I look!" Instead of being open to the friend's honest observation, you shut the other person down with an emphatic denial. Case closed! No discussion!

Defensiveness is a barrier that prevents us from being honest. It is a means of not allowing another person to speak truth into our lives. It often pushes those who love us most out of our lives. They may become reluctant to tell us the truth about ourselves in the future, so we become more disconnected from one another.

Defensiveness is a common problem in human relations and always impacts them negatively. However, defensiveness is even more destructive when a person suffers from unresolved pain and grief.

Pretense comes from the same root word as "pretend." A pretense is a false appearance or action intended to deceive. It is presenting ourselves as something other than what we are. A good friend might say, "You seem sad today." A pretentious response would be to put on a big smile and say, "I can't believe you'd say that! I've never felt better in my whole life."

We could create another example from Yvonne's life. A friend might say to Yvonne, "You must be very angry toward the person who molested you." If Yvonne wanted to be pretentious, she might respond, "Oh, it's really no big deal. I'm over it now and I'm doing fine!"

People use defenses and pretenses to protect themselves from having to face the truth.

Defenses and pretenses block those who care about them from helping. The consequences are dangerous, because people are driven away, causing the hurting person to be further disconnected from friends and loved ones. Increased disconnection leads to further isolation and more pain. And the cycle repeats.

A sure sign that people have engaged the grief process and are healing is that they feel less need to be defensive or pretentious. The defensive lies and denials are no longer needed. The truth becomes less frightening. We are not afraid that the truth will cause people to reject us.

If you are studying alone, use the spaces below. If you are studying in a small group, use the questions below for discussion.

1. *Can you recall a time(s) when you have been defensive? Describe.*

   _____

   _____

   _____

2. *Think about your feelings during the event described above. What caused you to act defensively?*

   _____

   _____

   _____

3. *Can you recall a time(s) when you acted pretentiously?*

_____

_____

_____

4. *Think about your feelings during the event described above. What caused you to act pretentiously?*

_____

_____

_____

THE FOURTH BIG LIE:
"Time heals all wounds."

This is one of the great lies among human beings. A more accurate statement would be "Time changes all wounds." A man had surgery on his knee to repair cartilage tears. In time, the wound from the surgery healed, but the damage in his knee increased. He developed acute arthritis and severe pain. Ultimately, he required knee replacement surgery. In his case, time did not heal the knee.

In Chapter 2 of *Healing Is a Choice*, we learned an important principle: "What is true of physical pain and the body is true for emotional pain and the soul." If time does not heal all physical pain, it's not likely to heal emotional pain.

Time changes wounds, but the changed wounds are usually bitterness, hatred, denial, rejection, and a cold absence of emotions.

What is accurate is that time heals all wounds that are appropriately treated. We need to spend time working on our past wounds. Both Karen and Yvonne were finally able to deal with their pain when they sought help from people trained to assist them.

This book is about healing choices. The most important choice is the powerful decision to act. Make a decision to stop being alone and suffering in silence. As long as you isolate yourself, there is not much chance for healing and growth. After all, you're stuck in the same place, with the same thoughts and the same patterns and the same behaviors. You're isolated! You simply cannot do the same things over and over and expect different results. The pattern must be interrupted. Make a decision to find the places where healing occurs. Make an appointment. Keep it. Do the work required. Being proactive leads to healing!

Your only other option is to remain in the same place and hope that time will cure you. Take it from thousands of people. Time will not heal you. Time will only make your pain last longer. Grieving your past and letting it go will heal you. Then, you can face the future with confidence.

We should be very thankful that we live in a time when Christian counseling is a viable option for so many people. Christian counseling is a discipline taught on scores of campuses. Christian psychiatrists, psychologists, and counselors are present in most localities across America, and more are being trained now. They are there to help you.

WHO ARE YOU?

At the beginning of this chapter, we read about Don Quixote, who wanted to "fight the unbeatable foe," "right unrightable wrongs," "live pure and chaste," "fight for the right," "be willing to march into hell for a heavenly cause," and "die in peace."

Quixote was a dreamer. His dreams were noble and righteous. They guided his life and inspired his quest.

Most of us have dreams and goals we establish early and try to fulfill. However, many of us get derailed along life's path. People hurt or abuse us. They take our dreams away from us. We suffer failures and losses. Some are so severely damaged that they get stuck in their pain for years, even decades. Sometimes we inflict pain, suffering, and defeat on ourselves as a result of bad choices.

It's important that we don't live with our losses and failures. We must remember that the One who loves us most has sent us a powerful message in His words to us: "Now glory be to God! By his mighty power at work within us, he is able to accomplish infinitely more than we would ever dare to ask or hope" (Eph. 3:20 NLT).

JOURNALING

Take a few minutes and review chapter 4. It is an important chapter with information to help hurting people and to help you minister to others. Have you experienced significant pain in your past? Did someone you loved cause it? Did the events leave you scarred? Have you repeatedly attempted to figure out a way to deal with it? At what point will you leave it behind and move on? Take time and write about your painful experiences and the impact they have had on your life.

_____

_____

_____

_____

_____

_____

_____

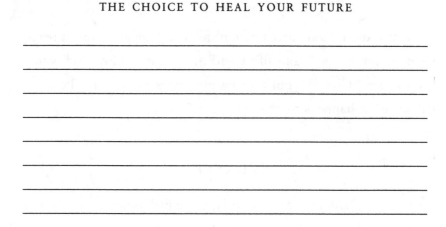

PRAYERFUL MEDITATION

Find a quiet, relaxing place where you are comfortable and uninterrupted. Ask the Holy Spirit to reveal pain you may still be experiencing from events in your past. Be patient and wait on the Spirit to speak to your mind. God wants you to acknowledge your pain, grieve over it, and have the courage to move boldly into your future. Remember that He has promised never to leave you or forsake you. Remember that He was despised and rejected, acquainted with grief. He knows how you feel. He knows the memories that continually torment you. He knows how you sometimes are triggered by events to remember past hurts. He has compassion on you and wants you to experience healing.

Are you willing? Will you face your pain, grieve, and walk into the light of a new life?

Ask the Holy Spirit to help you grieve. Let Him speak to your heart and mind. Then, ask Him to give you courage to change. Sit quietly for a few minutes and listen to the Holy Spirit. Thank God for the life He has given you. Thank Him because He is able to redeem the past.

Think about God's love and faithfulness. Imagine yourself being happy, unburdened, and filled with joy. That is how God wants you to be. "Give all your worries and cares to God, for he cares about what happens to you" (1 Pet. 5:7 NLT).

PRAYER

Heavenly Father, hear my prayer. I have endured so much pain for so long. I am worn out and want to move on with my life. Please help me. Send Your Holy Spirit to give me strength to deal with the wounds from my past. Help me to grieve instead of pushing things down deeper into my mind. Give me release from the emotional bondage I feel so often. Give me courage to allow others to help me. Lead me toward people who will accept and connect with me. Thank You for the challenge I have received from this chapter. I choose to take healing steps today. Please stay close to me as I take these steps. I truly want to be healed. You are the Great Physician. Do Your cleansing, redeeming, restorative work in me. Increase my confidence in You. Increase my faith. I give You my life; mind, soul, and spirit. Through Jesus Christ, my Healer. Amen.

REJOICE AND SING!

If you know this chorus, sing it to conclude your devotion. Its words of healing can strengthen your heart. If you don't know it, select a song or a hymn of your choice. Use it to worship God for a few minutes.

SAY THE NAME (OF JESUS)

Say the name of Jesus. Say the name of Jesus
Say the name so precious, No other name I know
That can calm your fears and dry your tears
And wipe away your pain
When you don't know what else to pray
When you can't find the words to say . . . say the name
Jesus, Jesus, Jesus, Jesus, He's gonna make a way.

5

THE FIFTH CHOICE:
The Choice to Help Your Life

THE FIFTH BIG LIE:
"I can figure this out by myself."

AT THIS POINT IN OUR JOURNEY THROUGH *HEALING IS A Choice*, you may have noticed a progression of healing steps, as follows:

- Chapter 1 established the importance of being connected to others.

- Chapter 2 explained the importance of feeling your life, especially your pain.

- Chapter 3 taught you to (a) investigate your life, and (b) search for truth in your life.

- Chapter 4 emphasized the importance of grieving your losses.

- Chapter 5 emphasizes the very important decision to reach outside yourself and help your life. You need help to heal. You need a healing team that includes yourself, appropriate friends and family, professional caregivers, someone from your faith community, and, most important, God. The truth you must face is that you are not going to heal yourself.

Writing in 1624, the pastor-poet John Donne penned these words: "No man is an island, entire of itself; every man is a piece of the continent, a part of the main."[1]

Donne's point is that no one can exist on his or her own, cut off from the rest of society. To use Donne's illustration, there are no human islands!

When Donne preached and wrote, most of Europe was moving toward isolationism. Nations were not seeking to be interconnected with one another. They were worn out from fighting and wanted to be left alone to form little "island-nations" all over Europe.

About that same time, Sir Thomas More wrote *Utopia*, which described an island-nation that prospered in its isolation. The irony of More's book was that the citizens of Utopia did not prosper because of being isolated. Rather, they prospered because they relied on one another. They were interconnected.

What is the purpose of this brief history lesson? I mention it because there is a strong comparison between John Donne's point and the theme of chapter 5.

You are not an island! You may have constructed a protective barrier around your life to protect yourself from future pain, but it is not helping you. You were not created to be alone, and you need to be connected to others in order to be healthy.

There is, however, one thing you can do to be healed. You must make the healing choice to reject isolationism and engage those who can help you.

One of the most important lessons to be learned in *Healing Is a*

Choice is that we need to be connected with others. None of us do very well with life alone. If we are dealing with serious emotional, spiritual, or psychological issues, withdrawing into isolation usually exacerbates the problems. Think back on the stories we've read. Rachael's condition improved as she began to connect with friends and, ultimately, good counselors. Laurie suffered because her husband failed to connect with her in the most vulnerable and painful time of her life. Karen withdrew into isolation due to lifelong rejection from her father. Yvonne spent more than forty years disconnected from her feelings and other people due to childhood abuse.

The truth is both simple and profound. We are not created to live isolated and alone. We are not meant to live without companionship. We are meant to live connected to family, friends, and others in an interdependent community.

If we withdraw and isolate ourselves, we suffer the consequences. When the investigation of our lives reveals that we need the help of others, then making a healing choice to reach outside and help our lives is the very best choice we can make. It takes courage to make that choice and commitment to see it through to its conclusion. Making such choices is a powerful way to help our lives.

THE FIFTH CHOICE:
The Choice to Help Your Life

A SICK MIND?

We live in a culture filled with people who desperately want to believe that, "I'm okay" and "you're okay!" Television hosts and celebrities tell us that all we need to live happy lives is to reach deep inside and draw out the emotional power. They tell us that "all the answers to your problems are inside you." Such cultural jargon usually does more harm than good. It's spoken out of context, misrepresented, misapplied, and often leads to compounded failure in people's lives.

Thus, *Healing Is a Choice* makes a very blunt statement on page 87. It reads, "In the midst of our happy talk, we need to accept the glaring reality that we each, to some degree or another, have a sick mind."

We rarely know how to solve our problems. None of us are perfect. We are all somewhat damaged. From a theological point of view, our damage results from "the Fall." As a result we have a sinful nature that needs healing. Jesus Christ, the Great Physician, heals our nature. From a sociological point of view, we are also somewhat damaged. No one had perfect parents or perfect adults around all the time. Consequently, we are somewhat damaged by those who raised us and those who interacted with our lives. Circumstances may have damaged us, as in the example of a child who becomes ill and must be bedridden for long periods of time, or a young person who is abused and must deal with the consequent pain for long years.

To some degree, our minds are sick and need healing.

THE ESSENTIAL CHOICE

We now reach a critical point in the book. We read that "right in front of every person is a path that is very wide and easy to follow" (Prov. 14:12, paraphrase.) The New Living Translation is even more emphatic: "There is a path before each person that seems right, but it ends in death." What's the point?

As we arrive at the decision to help our lives, we have a healing choice to make. We can take the wide, easy path. After all, it looks inviting and easy to manage. There don't seem to be any impediments in the way. We think, *This will be a breeze!*

But wait! People have taken that path before and gotten into deep trouble. That wide path is deceptive and filled with danger. We are warned not to take that path. But we think, *It's wide and easy. Why would we even consider another way?*

Jesus answered that question in Matthew 7: "You can enter God's kingdom only through the narrow gate. The highway to [destruction] is broad, and its gate is wide for the many who choose the easy way. But the gateway to life is small, and the road is narrow, and only a few ever find it" (vv. 13–14 NLT).

So, the choice is clearly stated. If we take the wide, easy path, we are headed for trouble. It is not the path of truth or wisdom. It does not lead us to God or the healing we need. It will not solve the problem of our sick minds. Consider some of the consequences listed in the book for those who take the wide, easy path:

- Microbiologists end up delivering mail (pp. 85–87).
- Pastors end up selling stocks and bonds.
- Married men end up having affairs.
- Women end up living like doormats.
- Geniuses end up behind bars.
- Wealthy people shoplift.
- Healthy people gain 180 pounds.
- Mothers hit the children they love.

The book offers more examples of people's lives falling apart as they head down the wide, easy path that Jesus called "the road to destruction." This is where our sick minds lead us.

How Do You Make Choices?

People make choices every day. Sometimes they are insignificant (What kind of toothpaste will I use?); at other times they are critical (Will I contact a Christian counselor to help me with my growing depression?). Each of us makes hundreds of decisions daily. How do you approach the decision-making process? Is it instinctive, deliberate, or both?

Answer the questions below. If you are studying in a small group, discuss them together.

1. *How do you determine the value of your choices? What makes some choices more important than others?*

_____

_____

_____

_____

2. *How many choices do you make in an average day that positively impact the quality of your life?*

_____

_____

_____

_____

3. *Do you have a process or strategy you use when making choices? Describe it.*

_____

_____

_____

_____

4. *List a few of the most important choices you've made in life. After each one, describe whether the choice was a good one or turned out to be a mistake.*

_____

_____

_____

_____

(a) _____

_____

(b) _____

_____

(c) _____

_____

(d) _____

_____

5. *Think of past choices. Perhaps you chose not to attend the state university in order to enroll at a Christian college. Perhaps you chose to give a year of your life to Christian service rather than accept a wonderful job offer you received. Maybe you chose to marry a dedicated Christian man rather than the non-believing man who swept you off your feet. Can you recall decisions you made that involved declining a great choice in order to make a choice in favor of something better?*

_____

_____

_____

_____

If we reject the choice of the wide and easy path, then what road should we take?

Clearly, the right option is what Jesus called the "narrow gate." The outcome of following Jesus' path leads to healing, health, a meaningful life, and joy. It's the road that ends in a good, productive life.

The discussion about choices of paths is addressed beautifully in a poem titled "The Road Not Taken," written by Robert Frost, one of America's greatest and most prolific poets. Read the poem carefully, perhaps more than once.

THE ROAD NOT TAKEN

Two roads diverged in a yellow wood,
And sorry I could not travel both
And be one traveler, long I stood
And looked down one as far as I could
To where it bent in the undergrowth;

Then took the other, as just as fair,
And having perhaps the better claim,
Because it was grassy and wanted wear;
Though as for that the passing there
Had worn them really about the same,

And both that morning equally lay
In leaves no step had trodden black.

Oh, I kept the first for another day!
Yet knowing how way leads on to way,
I doubted if I should ever come back.
I shall be telling this with a sigh
Somewhere ages and ages hence:
Two roads diverged in a wood, and I—
I took the one less traveled by,
And that has made all the difference.

6. *What is the message Frost is trying to convey in this poem?*

_____

_____

_____

_____

7. *Ask: Are Jesus and Robert Frost saying the same thing about the paths they recommend? Explain.*

_____

_____

_____

_____

IS SELF-HELP AN OPTION?

Choosing the right path to follow is an important choice, one that will either hurt our lives or heal them. Following the wide, easy path is a road to pain, not healing. People's lives fall apart on that road. They stumble into confusion and hopelessness.

Yet, thousands of people continue choosing the wide, easy path. Somehow, erroneously, they think that path will lead to health, or that they will magically find some sort of "self-help" solution to finally heal them. After all, isn't self-help a major industry in the United States? Yes, it is a big business generating huge amounts of money while healing a precious few people, if that! Just buy three books (you might not actually read them), twelve tapes, and attend four seminars. Then, hopefully, you will be instantly healed. That may be an oversimplification. However, a significant number of Americans think that self-help will cure all their ills! Actually, it creates more problems, because all people have really done is stay on that wide, easy path. They are still rejecting the hard, healing path.

Our sick minds that lead us down wrong paths are not going to somehow find the right path one day.

As *Healing Is a Choice* reminds us, "Self-help is not really self help at all. Self-help that really helps is God help, it is group help, it is expert help" (p. 88).

WARNING! No Help Leads to Poor Health, or Worse!

Here is a very important truth: We need help to get on the right path, because we are not capable of doing it alone. We must seek help beyond ourselves, and find the treatment we need. Otherwise, we could get sicker and increasingly harm our minds and bodies. The consequences are devastating.

Our bodies are not designed to tolerate the debilitating impact of unresolved conflicts and painful issues from our past. We sit in our chairs stewing over problems.

We can't seem to find solutions that work. We're frustrated, because we want to do something to solve our problems. Our bodies tense up, wanting to spring into action, but we sit immobilized. With no physical outlet, our bodies take a terrible hit, "like a chemistry set exploding in your head" (p. 89).

NOTE: For more details regarding the physical damage stress can produce, read page 89 again. You may also want to check the library or Internet for headings such as,

"How Does Stress Affect the Body?"
"Stress and Your Health,"
"The Effects of Chronic Stress on the Body."

There are common reasons why people do not seek the help they need, including:

1. They might feel embarrassed to seek help.

2. It would be viewed as a sign of weakness.

3. They would be "found out" (that they have a problem).

4. They've lost hope that anyone or anything can help.

There is no good reason to deny the help that is needed. In fact, we would actually call these excuses "denial." It never leads to healing. It always causes "illness."

The word picture painted in the book is a sad reminder of how ill people become when they are in denial. The description is: "the person limping past the counselor's office or the pastor's suite or the recovery group while saying to himself or herself, 'I am going to be just fine, one day, eventually, sooner or later, down the road, not too far away.'"

The truth is that we all have wounds, problems, and scars

of one kind or another. So, the sooner we get help, the quicker we will be healthy and whole.

"Denial" is just another term for self-deception. Denial says, "You're the only one in the world who feels this way or has this problem, and you shouldn't let anyone else know about it!"

Scripture has a response to denial. It says, "Trust in the LORD with all your heart; do not depend on your own understanding. Seek his will in all you do, and he will direct your paths. Don't be impressed with your own wisdom. Instead, fear the LORD and turn your back on evil" (Prov. 3:5–7 NLT).

These verses tell us to move away from our own under-standing. In its place, we should seek the help of competent, trained professionals, while also seeking the connectedness of good friends.

If you tore your knee cartilage, you'd see an orthopedic doctor as soon as possible. You'd have to in order to walk properly. If you had appendicitis, you'd see an internist or a surgeon who could remove it before it poisoned your body and threatened your life.

If you are dealing with emotional, spiritual, or psychological pain, you should follow the same strategy. As quickly as possible, seek professionals who can best help you.

CREATE A RESOURCE DIRECTORY: AN IMPORTANT WAY TO HELP

Here is an exercise that will be helpful for you individually, and perhaps for your church. Every church should maintain an up-to-date referral list of professionals who are trusted and can be rec-ommended as needed. Churches are often viewed as sources of information for people needing help. Churches are also primary centers of pastoral care. Even if you are receiving professional help, your church should be part of the healing team. You need a pastor who can offer solid biblical counsel and who can listen and pray with you. Churches and pastors are primary resources.

A directory makes referring easy. You will need to do some research, using a telephone book, medical directories, word-of-mouth recommendations, and firsthand information. Create as many categories as you need.

To begin building your directory, fill in the information below. Keep a personal copy and offer copies to your church and friends.

PSYCHOLOGISTS & PROFESSIONAL COUNSELORS

1. Name: _____ Phone 1: _____
   Address: _____ Phone 2: _____
   City: _____ State: _____
   Other Important Information: _____

2. Name: _____ Phone 1: _____
   Address: _____ Phone 2: _____
   City: _____ State: _____
   Other Important Information: _____

3. Name: _____ Phone 1: _____
   Address: _____ Phone 2: _____
   City: _____ State: _____
   Other Important Information: _____

CHRISTIAN COUNSELORS

1. Name: _____ Phone 1: _____

   Address: _____ Phone 2: _____

   City: _____ State: _____

   Other Important Information: _____

PSYCHIATRIST

1. Name: _____ Phone 1: _____

   Address: _____ Phone 2: _____

   City: _____ State: _____

   Other Important Information: _____

GRIEF SUPPORT

1. Name: _____ Phone 1: _____

   Address: _____ Phone 2: _____

   City: _____ State: _____

   Other Important Information: _____

GENERAL SUPPORT GROUPS (CANCER, DIABETES, HEART, ALZHEIMER'S, ETC.)

1. Name: _____ Phone 1: _____

   Address: _____ Phone 2: _____

   City: _____ State: _____

   Other Important Information: _____

2. Name: _____ Phone 1: _____

Address: _____ Phone 2: _____

City: _____ State: _____

Other Important Information: _____

_____

HOSPICE

1. Name: _____ Phone 1: _____

Address: _____ Phone 2: _____

City: _____ State: _____

Other Important Information: _____

CRISIS PREGNANCY

1. Name: _____ Phone 1: _____

Address: _____ Phone 2: _____

City: _____ State: _____

Other Important Information: _____

FINANCIAL ASSISTANCE AND COUNSELING

1. Name: _____ Phone 1: _____

Address: _____ Phone 2: _____

City: _____ State: _____

Other Important Information: _____

Substance Abuse Agencies and Groups

1. Name: _____ Phone 1: _____

   Address: _____ Phone 2: _____

   City: _____ State: _____

   Other Important Information: _____

Treatment

Acknowledging the genuine need for help in your life motivates you to put away the false hope of self-help and consider seeing a professional person who can guide and assist you in the healing process. The decision to seek help is an important healing choice. When you get to this point, treatment becomes a viable option.

The specific goal in treatment is to (a) grow in character, and (b) to become closer to Christlike living. However, there are other areas in which treatment would be beneficial. It could help resolve inward conflicts between Christlike character and contrary behaviors. It could also help you move toward consistency, doing the things you should do and rejecting the things you should not do. Consistency helps you live in conformity to your values, and to be the same person in private that you are in public.

What are some treatment options that can be pursued? They run from extreme to mild, depending on the need. In the extreme, psychiatric or psychological help might be valuable. Occasionally, but not often, hospitalization might be necessary. The more common treatments include medication to help you think clearly. One of the chief duties of psychiatrists is to prescribe and manage medication.

A marriage and family therapist can provide much-needed treatment for broken relationships. A pastor trained in counseling might be very helpful in one-to-one treatment. The pastor can also combine good counsel with the wisdom of Scripture and personal prayer.

Group therapy is usually a productive option, because it affords group members the advantage of discussing similar problems. Many churches also have various kinds of support groups available to the general public.

There are effective treatment options that cost little or nothing and have proven records of success. These include: Alcoholics Anonymous, Alanon, Celebrate Recovery, Divorce Recovery, and more. Helping your church develop a directory of resources like we described above will facilitate treatment and help.

A great advantage of participating in a support group is that you benefit from a structured treatment program while simultaneously enjoying more connectedness, which, as we have learned, is one of the more important aspects of our healing.

THE FIFTH BIG LIE:
"I can figure this out by myself."

Bluntly, the answer to this lie is, "No, you can't!" If you could figure it out, you would have by now. If you could heal yourself, you would already have done so. If you could make the pain go away, you would have done that long ago. You need help in the healing process. However, the one thing you can do is start the process, that is, make the healing choice to help your life.

The constant lie you will hear in your head is, *I can do this myself. I can do this myself.* You must tell yourself the truth. You can't. What you can do is run to those people and places that can help you heal.

Remember the last three lines in Frost's poem? They are:

> Two roads diverged in a wood, and I—
> I took the one less traveled by,
> And that has made all the difference.

The choice to help your life is the harder path, but it's the healing path.

Journaling

Take a few minutes and review chapter 5. It is a challenging chapter encouraging you to do the hard work of moving toward healing. Making such choices heals your life and changes your future. The good news is that Jesus is with you in the process. He understands our weaknesses and our reluctance to do what is best. Because He understands, He can truly help us. In your journal, explore the barriers we employ that keep us from being healed.

_____

_____

_____

_____

_____

_____

_____

_____

_____

PRAYERFUL MEDITATION

As before, find a quiet, relaxing place where you are comfortable and uninterrupted. Get a cup of coffee, some tea or hot chocolate. Ask the Holy Spirit to reveal places in your life where you may be reluctant to seek help. If you are stubbornly resisting what you know in your heart you should do, then repent and resolve to change.

If you need to pursue treatment for any reason, pray about the options you have.

Be patient and wait on the Spirit to speak to your mind. God wants to guide you in this process rather than have you marching out on your own. Remember, always, His promise never to leave you or forsake you. He loves you and cares about everything that occurs in your life. He is compassionate and full of grace and mercy.

Are you willing to help your life? Will you face your pain and walk into the light of a new life?

Ask the Holy Spirit to help you make this courageous choice. Let Him speak to your heart and mind. Sit quietly for a few minutes and listen to the Holy Spirit. Thank God for the gift of life He has given you.

PRAYER

Heavenly Father, hear my sincere prayer. I worry that I won't ever be well. I often feel as if I take one step forward and two steps back. I'm "up" one day and "down" the next. I've forgotten what consistency means.

Please help me get some balance and truth back into my life. Please give me hope that life will be better . . . soon. Please send Your Holy Spirit to do a deep, inner work in my soul. I want to laugh and feel lighthearted again. Please give me courage to seek the treatment I need. Give me more friends. I'm tired of being alone. Thank You for the challenge in this chapter. I hear it and will do my best to respond positively. Please stay close to me as I take more healing steps.

Increase my confidence in You. Increase my faith. I give You my life; mind, soul, and spirit. Through Jesus Christ, my Healer. Amen.

REJOICE AND SING!

If you know this hymn, sing it to conclude your devotion. The words can strengthen your heart. If you don't know it, select a song of your choice.

'TIS SO SWEET TO TRUST IN JESUS

'Tis so sweet to trust in Jesus,
Just to take Him at His word;
Just to rest upon His promise,
Just to know, Thus saith the Lord.

Chorus:
Jesus, Jesus, how I trust Him!
How I've proved Him o'er and o'er!
Jesus, Jesus, precious Jesus!
O for grace to trust Him more!

O how sweet to trust in Jesus,
Just to trust His cleansing blood:
Just in simple faith to plunge me
'Neath the healing, cleansing flood!

Yes 'tis sweet to trust in Jesus,
Just from sin and self to cease;
Just from Jesus simply taking
Life and rest, and joy and peace.

Chorus:
I'm so glad I learned to trust Him,
Precious Jesus, Savior, Friend;
And I know that He is with me,
Will be with me to the end.

6

THE SIXTH CHOICE:
The Choice to Embrace Your Life

THE SIXTH BIG LIE:
"If I just act as if there is no problem, it will finally go away."

REVIEW

We have learned some very important truths about healing in the first five chapters. It is important to reenforce what you've learned, so you can apply it to life. Before we move to chapter 6, let's do a review exercise. Read each statement below and fill in the blank:

1. One of the most important relational needs in the healing process is to be _____ with others.

2. We cannot heal if we are in denial. We must acknowledge the importance of feeling our lives, especially our _____.

3. It is necessary for us to investigate our lives and _____ for truth in them.

4. In order to move successfully into the future, we must do the important work of _____ our losses.

5. There comes a time in the healing process when we must reach outside ourselves and _____ our life.

The answers are found on the last page of this chapter. Check your responses to ensure that you have learned these important healing principles.

REDEMPTION!

Redemption is a wonderful word, one of the best in the English language. Even better, it is one of the greatest realities in life. God loves to redeem. It's one of His best things to do!

Scripture is filled with examples of redemption. Consider the story of Joseph.

After their father's death and burial, Joseph and his brothers returned to Egypt. The brothers were afraid Joseph would punish them for the way they mistreated him as a young boy. They had been very jealous of Joseph. Back in Egypt, they told Joseph that their father had left a message asking Joseph not to harm them. Then, they begged Joseph for forgiveness for what they had done long ago. Finally, the brothers went to Joseph, bowed low in submission, and volunteered to be his slaves.

Joseph was overcome with emotion and wept. He told them not to be afraid, because he would not harm them. He said, "'Am I God, to judge and punish you? As far as I am concerned, God turned into good what you meant for evil. He brought me to the high position I have today so I could save the lives of many people. No, don't be afraid. Indeed, I myself will take care of you and your families.' And he spoke very kindly to them, reassuring them" (Gen. 50:19–21 NLT).

That story is a perfect description of redemption. What Joseph's brothers meant for evil God turned to good! He redeemed Joseph's situation.

Joseph's brothers deserved to be punished for what they did. They had hoped Joseph would be killed. As it was, he suffered much as a result of their treachery. The brothers should have been severely punished.

However, Joseph forgave them! Instead of punishment, he welcomed them back into the family. He redeemed their situation by paying the price of forgiveness, so that their relationship could be restored.

The theme of the greatest story ever told is redemption. It is the story of Jesus Christ, who willingly gave His life to redeem us, so we could become the sons and daughters of God.

Life is filled with stories of redemption. A father gives his life to save a drowning child. A mother works long hours in a tough job for many years, so her handicapped daughter can attend a special school and learn to live a normal life.

Culture is filled with examples of redemption. We find them in literature, music, media, and daily life. Scores of movies have redemptive themes, including: *It's a Wonderful Life, A Christmas Carol, The Shawshank Redemption, Dead Man Walking, Ground Hog Day, A River Runs Through It, The Passion of the Christ,* and many more.

Literature provides its share of redemption stories as well. Think of Victor Hugo's *Les Miserables,* and C. S. Lewis's The Chronicles of Narnia. More books have been written with redemptive themes than we can possibly mention.

WHY WE NEED REDEMPTION

There is a kind of redemption that is objective and connected theologically to salvation. It has to do with an event, the redemptive work of Christ on the cross. Every person needs to experience that redemption. It saves us and incorporates us into the family of God.

However, there is another aspect of redemption that speaks to all of life. It is a reflection of what Christ did on the cross. It works in and through us, so that we have the power to be redemptive toward people and situations. It is a process more than an event.

Every person needs to experience that kind of redemption, too. We need it because we are prone to fail. We make mistakes, suffer unintended failures, and sometimes deliberately hurt others. To be blunt, we tell lies, and we are not always honest in our relationships. We need some means to deal with all these failures. Redemption gives us that and helps to heal the deep pains of life.

We need it because we can become the victim of other people's choices, and that hurts deeply.

This aspect of redemption provides the strength and ability we need to forgive one another.

Redemption is an important way of establishing a relationship with God and with others. Thus it is a vital part of the healing process. To accept redemption is a powerful healing choice. To be redemptive is a powerful healing act.

The most important healing decision we can make is to accept the redemption that God offers us through Jesus Christ. The moment we make that decision, we move onto the road of recovery and healing. Healing may be a long way ahead, but we've finally arrived on the right road!

Redemption is God's way of turning into good what was meant for evil (Exod. 50:19–21).

Redemption needs a reason. It is a response to something bad that has happened; sin, defeat, failure, betrayal, molestation, broken relationships, and rejection from loved ones. It allows us to forgive, restore, and have hope. It calls out to us to do the right thing.

We can be sure that when redemption is at work in our lives, things are moving in a healing direction.

A Tough Journey, a Healing Arrival

This chapter offers us a very personal and poignant story of how powerful redemption can be. Read again pages 103–9 in *Healing Is a Choice*.

This story of divorce, grief, and recovery asks an important question: "Does God use tragedy?" The answer is, "Absolutely!" How does He use it? He redeems it!

We are all broken in some way. We all experience failures of various kinds. After a great tragedy, redemption is our best hope at becoming useful again. It means that God can still use us in spite of our history or circumstances. Why? Because He redeems both! Remember: "God turns into good what is meant for evil" (Gen. 50:19–21 NLT, paraphrase).

The story in chapter 6 begins when divorce papers were served. It felt terrible for everyone involved. It had the potential to be controversial, and to a few people, it was. It took a while to fully accept the awful truth. I was a divorced minister. I hated it, but I had to face it. I knew people would be talking about it without any input from me to help them understand.

The lessons I learned through this process were truths that can help anyone going through a crisis, suffering a tragedy, or enduring failure. Ultimately, these lessons helped me arrive at a good place.

Lesson One: "Face, Then Embrace"

If we are going to heal, we must make the choice to face the truth of what is happening to us, accept and embrace it.

1. *Can you remember a time in your life when you were forced to face a situation that seemed overwhelming and out of control? Describe how you felt in the space provided.*

_____

_____

_____

2. *How did you "face it"?*

_____

_____

_____

3. *How did you recover?*

_____

_____

_____

When it comes to facing and embracing our problems, we really have no choice. The problems exist in reality, which we cannot change. Embracing them means we are accepting reality as it is. We may not like it or want it, but anything other than acceptance is denial. We have learned in *Healing Is a Choice* that denial is a destructive barrier to healing. Tolerating it is a willful choice against healing!

Having accepted a reality we cannot change, it is important to embrace it. Why would we want to embrace something that is painful? On the surface, that seems like a poor choice.

Why would anyone want to "embrace" divorce? Being divorced means that one's identity is forever changed. It's not unlike a person who loses their leg in an automobile accident. No one desires that, but it happens, and once it does, it cannot be denied or rejected without psychological consequences. The healing choice is to embrace the reality before us and accept that we are forever changed.

Embracing reality means we move into the experience rather than hide from it. It also means we accept the fact that our identity has changed in some significant way. That may be an undesired reality. You didn't want it, but it's there!

Think of some undesired reality you have faced. Answering the following four questions will help you examine your feelings and thoughts as you reflect on it. It is important to "self-examine," so that you don't get "stuck" in negative emotions.

1. *Recall a time in your life when an undesired reality was thrust upon you. Perhaps it was a sudden, severe illness in your family, or even a death. Maybe it was the loss of a job, a divorce, or financial failure. How did you feel?*

---

2. *How did you respond to the event? Did you reject it at first or try to deny it was happening to you?*

_____

_____

_____

3. *Have you been able to embrace it? If so, how long did it take? Or, are you still in the process of accepting and embracing it?*

_____

_____

_____

4. *Since you embraced the new reality in your life, how have you felt?*

_____

_____

_____

Lesson Two: "We're All Just So Screwed Up!"

Are you offended by the term "screwed up"? Some of you may be. However, you might be surprised to learn that the phrase is listed in the Oxford Dictionary. It means "bungle" or "mess." Those two words have a number of meanings, including: trouble, mismanagement, work clumsily, state of confusion, and embarrassment. Put all those words together and you get "screwed up"!

It would be an error to say that we all have our "act together." Most of the time, the exact opposite is true. Very few of us have our act together. Add to that the fact that human beings are an unpredictable lot. We do some unexpected and weird things without warning.

Our lives are not always as organized and well-managed as we'd prefer. Often, old wounds and emotional scars keep us "screwed up" and disoriented.

We suffer that condition due to sudden, violent, even evil acts perpetrated on us by people whose agenda was to harm. It wasn't so much what we did, as what people did to us. It's not surprising that some of us would be "screwed up." What is surprising is that some of us can cope at all. Sadly, many people can't.

We marry individuals who we intuitively know are not compatible. We damage significant relationships, thus isolating ourselves. We make choices that result in long-term negative consequences. We're often "screwed up" from pretending that everything in our life is perfect when, clearly, it is not. We cover our pain with facades.

By definition, a facade is a deceptive outward appearance. In ancient Greek theaters, the masks worn by actors were facades. If they wanted to convey happiness, they wore a smiling facade. If they wanted to convey sadness, they wore a frowning one.

People still wear facades every day, often to mask what is really true inside them. They are covering up, hiding their real selves. Such masquerading is another way of being "screwed up" and pretending to be something other than what we really are.

Chapter 5 taught us that defenses and pretenses are debilitating obstacles to healing. They keep us in bondage. In contrast, Scripture teaches that "the truth will set you free" (John 8:32 NLT). Facades and lies imprison us in jails of our own design.

The good news of the gospel is that redemption is available. No one has to stay in the condition in which they find themselves. Everyone has free choices to make each day that either heal us or hurt us.

Regarding divorce, facing and embracing it means that we refuse to live in denial. We remove the facades and defense mechanisms, and accept reality. With no facades to wear, we can connect with people as we truly are, in an authentic and personal way. We can accept the tag of "divorce," being a single parent, and the stigma people sometimes attach to us.

Lesson Three: "As If It Were Meant to Be"

God specializes in paradoxes (opposites that nevertheless are true). An example is: "Whoever wants to be a leader among you must be your servant, and whoever wants to be first must become your slave. For even I, the Son of Man, came here not to be served but to serve others, and to give my life as a ransom for many" (Matt. 20:26–28 NIV).

It is paradoxical how often God's people end up in jail. Good people don't belong in jail. Jail is for the "bad guys," not God's elect. Yet, it happens, repeatedly. Consider a few of God's "jailbirds."

Joseph spent thirteen years in prison, a significant portion of his life. How could that possibly have been a good thing? Most of us would rail against such injustice. We'd demand a new trial. We'd hire expensive lawyers and protest. There would be a letter-writing campaign, and we'd inundate the legislature with mail. But Joseph accepted it and embraced it. He actually turned it into a positive experience in the long run, thus redeeming his situation.

116

In retrospect, we realize that God was in it. Surely God did not condone the injustice of it all, but once it happened, He was there unfolding His will as if it were meant to be.

Paul was familiar with jails. His heart's desire was to preach the gospel throughout the entire world. Instead, he spent an undue amount of time behind bars! Certainly, God's will for Paul was for him to teach, preach, and evangelize in as many places as possible. Prison kept interfering. However, once in prison, God was always there, unfolding His will as if it were meant to be!

Paul used his prison time to do a very simple thing, writing letters. Remarkably, those letters from jail became the backbone of the New Testament. We still read them today! In retrospect, it seems as if it was meant to be.

Chuck Colson is a contemporary example. He was sent to prison for committing crimes related to the Watergate scandal during Richard Nixon's presidency. Colson fell from the highest position of power to a dismal prison cell. While there, he gave his life to Christ, and created one of the greatest prison ministries in the world. God's desire was not that Colson would be disgraced and imprisoned, but once it happened, God began unfolding the events of his life as if it were meant to be.

Joni Eareckson Tada is another example. Her story involves a prison of a different kind. It has no bars. It is the prison of her disability. Joni broke her neck in a diving accident and became a quadriplegic as a result of one error in judgment. God did not intend for her to be imprisoned in a wheelchair, but once it happened, He turned it into something good, as if it was meant to be.

God wants to teach us that He can work with our failures, liabilities, and limitations, if we will embrace them and let Him lead.

Joseph could have spent thirteen years being bitter and angry. Paul could have become frustrated to the point of depression. Colson could have become hardhearted and vindictive. Joni might have given up hope and languished flat on her back. However, God had plans for them, as if it were meant to be all along.

Even in divorce, God is at work, changing circumstances, guiding, and empowering us. Most of all, He is redeeming, turning bad to good.

These examples give us hope that God can and will redeem the failures, mistakes, omissions, difficulties, health issues, and liabilities of our lives.

1. *Think of a time in your life when something happened that felt awful. It may have felt unfair. You didn't deserve it, but it happened, and you had to deal with it. Describe the event and the feeling you experienced.*

   _____

   _____

   _____

2. *Describe something good that resulted from the events described in #1.*

   _____

   _____

   _____

No matter how terrible your circumstances are, God is with you. You may have been abused as a child, betrayed by a spouse, molested by a relative, rejected by a father, or locked in an emotional prison filled with pain. The good news is that God never left or forsook you. He loves you, and He is working to turn all those trials and hurts into something good, as if they were meant to be from the beginning. Whatever horrible thing is threatening your life, allow God to work with it. He is the God of redemption. It is one of His best things to do!

Lesson Four: "Radical Adjustment of Expectations"

At some point in our lives, most of us will need to radically adjust our expectations. We will experience obstacles, limitations, and circumstances that demand it. Things we once did without a second thought will no longer be options for us. If we don't make adjustments, we will be continually frustrated and angry.

We will reach an age where we can't run a twelve-mile marathon. We won't be able to eat the way we did at twenty-six years old. We will require more sleep. Our energy levels will decrease, if they haven't already! At work, we will be surpassed by the "young turks."

If we don't make adjustments in our expectations, we will live with constant frustration. We will become emotionally and psychologically unhealthy.

However, we have a better option. We can make a healing choice to embrace life as it is. We can make needed adjustments, so we can live life to its fullest. We will do life in new ways, but it will be life, and it can be good!

Our fear is that any change or adjustment in expectations will diminish us. We view this kind of change as diminishment. We see it as failure and loss.

However, there is overwhelming evidence that changes in life patterns are not the same as diminishment. As we get older, changes are important if we want to live successfully.

We must embrace the life God gives us at whatever stage we are in. The adjustments we make are necessary losses.

We must accept our own humanity, with its limitations, and allow God to work with us in whatever circumstances we find ourselves.

Lesson Five: "Embracing the Abrasive"
Embracing and accepting life includes dealing with people who make life difficult. That's not great news, but it is a fact of life. *Healing Is a Choice* names these people. They are called "Grace Growers" and "Character Builders" for obvious reasons.

When we see these folks coming, we want to "run for the hills." They drain us of energy and cry on our shoulders. Their problems are never resolved, and they bounce from one caregiver to another, wearing people out.

What are we to do with these people? Why are they in our lives?

In another example of divine paradoxes, God brings these people into our lives to shape our character. Abrasive people may offend us, but they also make us better people.

God allows such encounters to advance His purposes in us. "Grace Growers" build strength in us we might otherwise never experience. "Character Builders" toughen us, so we can endure the challenges of life as God uses us. David would not have become the man he was, except for his struggles with Saul.

Remember that Jesus said, "If any of you wants to be my follower, you must put aside your selfish ambition, shoulder your cross daily, and follow me. If you try to keep your life for yourself, you will lose it. But if you give up your life for me, you will find true life. And how do you benefit if you gain the whole world but lose or forfeit your own soul in the process?"(Luke 9:23–25 NLT).

Healing Is a Choice offers this paragraph: "Remember the story of David and the giant? If David had taken on a third grader, I don't think we would have heard much about it. The bigger the challenge, the more God can do with it, even when the worst outcome occurs. Alter your expectations and embrace the life you have, and you will live far beyond the expectations you had before. It just won't be in the form you originally wanted."

Think about the above paragraph for a few minutes. Let it roll around in your mind. Consider each sentence. Then, react to the paragraph by expressing your thoughts below:

_____

_____

_____

_____

_____

_____

_____

_____

_____

THE SIXTH BIG LIE:

"If I just act as if there is no problem, it will finally go away."

The sixth big lie reminds us of pretenses. It encourages us to pretend that we have no problems, when in fact we are struggling mightily with them. This lie promises that by pretending, our problems will go away. That's not just a lie; it's a whopper of a lie!

If we pretend we have no problems, the ones we have and are ignoring will increase. The result will be more misery.

This lie is also an unhealthy crutch. You grow to depend on it. You wake each morning hoping this is the day it will come true. The lie becomes your constant companion. It keeps making grandiose promises to you each day, only to disappoint and frustrate in the end.

Problems rarely go away by themselves. No amount of pretending can hide the fact that this lie disappoints you day after day after day.

The answer is to overwhelm the lie with the truth. Face your problems. Don't try to cover them up or deny them. Call them what they are. Shine the light on them. Ask God to help you overcome them.

Remember that healing is a choice. It is God's choice, but we have a part to play.

We can stand in the way of healing by continuing to believe the big lie. However, there is a better option. We can embrace the life we have, with all its difficulties and challenges, and remember that God is redeeming us and our circumstances. God loves to redeem. Its one of His best things to do!

JOURNALING

Take a few minutes and review chapter 6. Note the strong emphasis on redemption. Take some time as you journal and record your thoughts about what redemption means to you. Consider the love of God that created redemption and offers it to us.

Review the big lie and think about how it tries to diminish the power of redemption.

Remember that healing is a choice, and redemption is one type of healing. How can you appropriate God's redemptive work into your life?

_____

_____

_____

_____

_____

_____

_____

_____

_____

_____

_____

_____

_____

_____

PRAYERFUL MEDITATION

As before, find a quiet, relaxing place where you are relaxed and uninterrupted. Maybe you have selected a favorite place by this time. Sit in a comfortable chair. Take a few minutes and think about the blessings of God. Ask the Holy Spirit to give you a genuine understanding of redemption. Think about how redemption changes your life and gives you hope. Remember that redeeming is God's best thing to do. He wants you to experience it at its deepest levels. Remember, also, that God redeems lives and circumstances.

Think about the sixth big lie. Have you ever believed it? If you believe this lie, you will be engaging in magical thinking, not spiritual truth.

Your quality of life depends on trusting God, not hoping your problems will just go away.

God's Holy Spirit will direct you into all truth. Listen to Him. Inculcate His truth into your mind and heart.

God is always working in your life. As you look back, even being mindful of your struggles, you will see that your life is just as it was meant to be!

Be patient and wait on the Spirit to speak to your mind. Remember, always, His promise never to leave you or forsake you. He loves you and cares about everything that occurs in your life. He is compassionate and full of grace and mercy.

Are you willing to embrace your life? Will you accept it and use it for God's glory? It doesn't matter that you are scared and wounded. He can still use you. Thank God for the gift of life He has given you.

PRAYER

Heavenly Father, hear my earnest prayer. I want to experience redemption at its deepest level. I worry that I may take it for granted and not appreciate the sacrifice that appropriates my redemption. Help me to realize that the life You have given me is good. Help me to remember that, regardless of what has happened to me in the past, You can always redeem it and make my life pleasing to You. I sometimes struggle with believing that You have totally forgiven me. I need help with that. I also have trouble believing that You still love me, considering some of the things I've done. I am not worthy of Your redemption, but I desperately need and desire it. Help me to believe and trust in the fact that You are working in my life every day, shaping it into Your plan. Help me not to resist that. Please send Your Holy Spirit to do a deep, inner work in my soul. I want to be genuinely filled with Your Spirit. Thank You for the challenge in this chapter. I hear it and will do my best to respond positively. Please stay close to me as I take more healing steps. Make me bolder and more attentive to Your will. I give You my life; mind, soul, and spirit. Through Jesus Christ, my Friend. Amen.

Rejoice and Sing!

If you know this hymn, sing it to conclude your devotion. If you don't know it, read the words and meditate on them.

I SURRENDER ALL

All to Jesus, I surrender;
All to Him I freely give;
I will ever love and trust Him,
In His presence daily live.

Refrain

I surrender all, I surrender all,
All to Thee, my blessed Savior,

I surrender all.

All to Jesus I surrender;

Humbly at His feet I bow,

Worldly pleasures all forsaken;

Take me, Jesus, take me now.

Refrain

All to Jesus, I surrender;

Make me, Savior, wholly Thine;

Let me feel the Holy Spirit,

Truly know that Thou art mine.

Refrain

All to Jesus, I surrender;

Lord, I give myself to Thee;

Fill me with Thy love and power;

Let Thy blessing fall on me.

Refrain

All to Jesus I surrender;

Now I feel the sacred flame.

O the joy of full salvation!

Glory, glory, to His Name!

Refrain

ANSWERS TO REVIEW ON PAGE ONE:

1. connected 2. pain 3. search 4. grieving 5. help

7

THE SEVENTH CHOICE:
The Choice to Forgive

THE SEVENTH BIG LIE:
"Forgiveness is only for those who deserve it or earn it."

ALEXANDER POPE, THE EIGHTEENTH-CENTURY ENGLISH POET and essayist, penned these words: "To err is human; to forgive, divine."

Read that phrase several times. Read it again. Repeat it aloud. Let it sink deeply into your mind. Ponder its meaning.

Exercise #1: Defining the Phrase
In your own words, describe the meaning of the above phrase.

_____

_____

_____

_____

_____

_____

_____

_____

_____

Pope realized that all human beings make mistakes and experience failures. It is to be expected. It is the common human experience.

We even have a category for some accidents, "human error." It means an accident was not caused by mechanical or system failure. The person guiding the endeavor caused it. Whatever depends on human beings for control will, at some point, experience a failure due to human error. Why? Because "to err is human."

Pope also realized that without forgiveness, there is no way to deal with human error. Consider a relatively common situation in America. A young teenage driver hops into a car and heads for his best friend's house. Driving through a residential area, the young driver diverts his eyes from the road to find his favorite CD. In that instant, he fails to notice the child running into the road to retrieve a ball. Had the teen been focused on the road, he could have stopped in time. Because he looked away, he hits the child, who dies on the way to the hospital.

How are human beings able to deal with such tragedy? The young teen may be forever trapped in a dungeon of guilt. In an instant, the child's family is tragically and forever changed. Grief and anger become their constant companions. The teen driver and the child's parents scream out to God, "Why did You let this happen?" But it was not God's fault. It was the result of human error, in this case, a reckless mistake. The young driver took his eyes off the road for one moment and life changed forever. "To err is human." Be it an accident or a choice, we are all prone to err.

We cannot change realities like the one described above. What's done is done.

However, we desperately need some way of dealing with human

error. How can we live with tragedies of our own making? How can we deal with human error and failure?

This chapter in *Healing Is a Choice* challenges the reader to make choices to forgive. Forgiveness is the most powerful and successful tool we have for dealing with human failure.

The remainder of this lesson is designed to help you make forgiving choices, even in circumstances that seem unforgivable. It is written to show you that forgiveness is the only way to combat the anger, bitterness, and resentment resulting from human failure.

Are you ready? No doubt some of you who are reading this are beginning to feel tense and reluctant to continue. You know you need to forgive someone, or perhaps several people. You think about it often. But you can never quite bring yourself to do it.

This is God's time for you. It is a divine appointment. You are not reading this chapter by accident. Therefore, take a moment to pray before you go farther. Use the prayer below. The next few minutes can be transforming and liberating for you. The Holy Spirit is present. He will help you.

Loving, forgiving Father, I know I am not reading this chapter by accident. You have brought me to this time and place. I need forgiveness, and I need to forgive. I especially need to do this now. I've put it off too long. I need the strength and power of Your Holy Spirit. Please fill me now with His presence and power to do what is clearly Your will. I open my heart and my mind to hear, so please speak to me. I offer my will to obey, so please teach me. I offer my life to You, so please lead me. I trust in the redeeming, forgiving power of Christ my Lord. Amen.

The Most Dangerous Thing on Earth: Justifiable Resentment

What is the most dangerous thing on earth? A virus? A terrorist? An earthquake?

An angry mob? No. The most dangerous thing on earth is a particular attitude we might call "justifiable resentment."

What is resentment? By definition it is "indignation or ill will felt as a result of a real or imagined grievance."[1]

Resentment is a common experience. Far too many people live with it. Some folks are consumed with it. They seem to resent everything, from paying taxes to paying tithes, from the price of gas to the price of groceries, from politicians to preachers. They resent their neighbors and their employers. They may resent their spouses. As their resentment increases, they begin to make negative judgments about those whom they resent. Eventually, they become negative about everything. Deep resentments sour their lives to the point where no one wants to be with them. The emotional price is too high. Sadly, we all know people like that and we struggle in our relationship with them. In an attempt to help them change, we'll say, "Try not to be so negative," "Look for the good in people and accept them as they are," or "If you'd make a few changes, you'd enjoy life more."

There is a particular kind of resentment that can do irreparable harm. It's a resentment based on a real, horrible event. It is real damage inflicted on a real victim by a real perpetrator. The damage done to the victim is so horrible and painful that it becomes the predominant event in their lives. They experience anger and develop grudges. Because they were victimized, their anger and resentment seem justifiable. In *Healing Is a Choice*, this type of suffering is referred to as "justifiable resentment."

We read stories about such people experiencing justifiable resentment and think, *They have a right to feel as they do*, and *If it were me, I'd feel the same way*! All the evidence supports their anger, bitterness, and unwillingness to forgive. Theirs is not some free-floating resentment. It is resentment for good reason! An event occurred in space and time. It can be documented, and worse, it can be remembered. It was horrible, and the saddest part of it is that it happened to you!

Because you are a victim, friends, family, and professional care-givers will sympathize with you. No one doubts your story or your feelings. Everyone is very supportive. Some friends will even tell you it's "okay" to feel resentful. Thus, it is easy to embrace and nurture your grudge.

Despite the support you receive from family and friends, justifiable resentment will seriously damage your life. It is as if there is a terror-ist inside you trying to "blow you apart." It deprives you of joy. It diminishes your life. It hurts your relationship with God. The worst consequence is that it keeps you in bondage to an event. Your life becomes about one thing.

Exercise #2: Exploring Your Resentment

1. *Let me ask you to do a brave and personal thing. If there is an event in your life about which you feel justifiable resentment, take a few minutes and do the exercise below. (If you've never experienced such an event, think of a friend or a loved one and write about them.) Describe the event. What caused your resentment?*

_____

_____

_____

_____

2. *Explain how you justify your resentment.*

_____

_____

_____

_____

We know it is unhealthy and unspiritual to be resentful. Resentment does us great harm and usually hurts us more than those for whom we hold the grudge.

"Justifiable resentment" is an "oxymoron" (i.e., a contradiction in terms). It makes no sense to hold a grudge and justify it at the same time.

In the space below, develop a "plan of action" that frees you from both the resentment and the temptation to justify it. (Remember, this can only involve your actions. You cannot count on the other person to respond or do the right thing. The issue is what can YOU do?)

_____

_____

_____

_____

Healing Is a Choice encourages us to break free from the bondage of "justifiable resentment." With God's help, you really can let go of it and experience healing. Remember, healing is a choice you make. In this case it is a choice to forgive, let go, and heal.

That brings us back to the second part of Alexander Pope's powerful statement, "to forgive, [is] divine." If you can forgive, you can heal. In fact, if you will forgive, you will wake up one morning and realize that your life has changed. You will realize that you are no longer enslaved by one event in your past. The past will no long terrorize you, as it has most of your life. The healing choice to forgive is yours.

THE PHYSIOLOGY OF FORGIVENESS

David wrote, "When I refused to confess my sin, I was weak and miserable, and I groaned all day long" (Ps. 32:3 NLT). The New International Version is a bit more graphic: "When I kept silent, my bones wasted away through my groaning all day long."

David was expressing what we know to be true about the physiological impact of psychological pressures. Resentment, guilt, repressed feelings, and sin combine to create physical and emotional illnesses in us.

Consider the following report from researchers in Tennessee. They surveyed more than one hundred students who felt they had experienced an incident of serious personal betrayal. The researchers determined which of the students had the most forgiving personalities and which had less-forgiving personalities. Finally, researchers gathered students in a lab, where their vital signs were monitored. The students were asked to recall the incident or incidents of betrayal. Results confirmed that students with forgiving personalities recorded lower blood pressure and heart rate levels than the less-forgiving students. Additionally, signs of sympathetic nervous system arousal (stress response) that elevated during betrayal discussions returned to normal quicker in "forgiving" students than it did in the "less-forgiving types."[2] As a result of their work, they suggested that forgiveness may not only be divine, but also a good way to stay healthy.

Physicians and psychologists also confirm reports like the one above. They are substantiating what clergy and people of faith have always intuitively known. Forgiveness is a key to preventing many illnesses and reducing stress. If you can forgive, you can recover, embrace your life, and move confidently into the future.

Holding grudges, being resentful, staying angry, and repeatedly rehearsing past events in your mind are a certain prescription for illness. Your body will suffer the consequences. Your mental health will be impacted. With enough stress, you could even experience chronic disease. You may experience hormonal changes that lead to cardiac disease and impaired immune function. Your heart will suffer. Your misery will increase.

In contrast, forgiveness is a healer. It allows us to deal with our past mistakes and sins by accepting the forgiveness that God offers. It allows us to deal with our present, which is the theme of this chapter. It teaches us that there is no need to hold grudges or nurture resentments. We can release them as we extend forgiveness.

Forgiveness also allows us to deal with our future. Because we have been forgiven, we have hope now, and in the future. We can anticipate new friends and more fellowship, because we have learned how to forgive.

The good news is that every one of us has the power to make a free choice to forgive. We don't have to hold on to resentment. We can choose to be forgivers.

Resentment builds walls between people. Forgiveness tears down those walls and unites people.

Take a moment and imagine how dramatically the world would change if people suddenly decided to extend forgiveness to one another. Racial prejudices would fade. Rival African tribal groups would stop killing one another. Irish Protestants and Catholics might learn to live in peace. Arabs and Jews could live together in Palestine. Shi'ites and Sunnis might discover that they really are brothers. Murder rates would go down. The Chinese and Japanese would give up their ancient rivalries. Families could be reunited and restored. Who knows, Republicans and Democrats might even get along!

THE HARDEST PERSON TO FORGIVE

No discussion of forgiveness would be complete without addressing the subject of forgiving oneself. Thousands of people live in prisons of their own making. How does that happen?

In some families, mothers and fathers had extraordinarily high expectations for their children. Some parents had unreasonable expectations. In such an environment children are almost never able to satisfy their parents. Thus, they often fail. In many cases they are punished for their failures. Being young and naive, the children redouble their efforts to please their parents, only to fail repeatedly. These children grow up wounded and damaged. They take responsibility for never pleasing their unreasonable parents. Deep inside, they resent being raised in such a rigid environment, lacking in affection and patience. They long for someone, anyone, who will show them affection. Thus, they run to the first person who will show them genuine affection, or they will move toward what is familiar, marrying someone like their parents.

In families like the one described, children rarely blame their parents. Rather, they blame themselves. When they grow into adulthood, they have to make a healing choice: will I continue to accept responsibility for rigid, unaffectionate parents, or will I forgive myself and move on?

You may need to forgive yourself for taking all the blame in your life. You may need to forgive yourself for stuffing away the issues you have with your parents. You may need to forgive yourself for trying to be perfect, rather than normal.

You need to forgive yourself and break free from the emotional prison you inhabit. Forgiving yourself allows you to be a normal person with normal flaws. Remember that God did not create any of us to be perfect. He created us to be His children. God loves us more than our earthly parents or anyone else could ever imagine. "The unfailing love of the LORD never ends! By his mercies we have been kept from complete destruction. Great is his faithfulness; his mercies begin afresh each day" (Lam. 3:22–23 NLT).

All our stories are different. Some of us lived relatively normal and stable lives. We experienced our parents' affection in a caring environment. However, not everyone was so fortunate! Some of us experienced horrific experiences in life, so traumatic that they cannot be spoken and are never shared with anyone.

The road to freedom and recovery is to make a healing choice to seek help and support. If people do not get appropriate help, they forever allow their past to control them. *Healing Is a Choice* contains so much encouraging information to guide you in the process of working through your past. Use the advice in the book. Consider it God's personal road map to recovery. It is there for you.

To Forgive or Not Forgive, That Is the Question

Not everyone in the world is predisposed toward forgiveness. Certainly, Christians encourage it, and most people embrace forgiveness as a cultural value. But there are countries and cultures in the world that advocate vengeance rather than forgiveness. For them, the goal is not to reconcile or make peace, but to "even the score" or "get even." Ancient Babylonian law taught the same thing. It required "an eye for an eye, and a tooth for a tooth: whatever you did to me, I'll do to you!" One person noted that the only good that comes from such a legal system is a "sightless, toothless" world!

In cultures where vengeance is accepted, people think, *Why forgive?* What good can come from that? The important thing is to get even. Someone killed my son or daughter, so I will kill their son or daughter. The sad truth in such cultures is that justice is never done. The only result is that two people end up dead rather than one.

However, it is necessary to ask the question "Why forgive?" The purpose of forgiveness is not just to deal with an offender. Rather, it is also about freeing victims from grudges and resentments that keep them chained to the past. When you choose to forgive, you unlock the chain and set yourself free.

People often say, "I'll be over the pain and abuse when the perpetrator says he's sorry." That dooms the victim to remain in bondage to the past. The perpetrator may never apologize, then what? Is the victim forever bound? Perhaps. However, by forgiving, you can be free. Lewis Smedes wrote, "When we forgive, we set a prisoner free and discover that the prisoner we set free is us."

Exercise #3: Forgiving Yourself and Forgiving Others

Often, the baggage from our past weighs heavily on our minds. You may recall painful encounters and feel guilty as a result. Perhaps you lied to a friend, hurt someone deeply, or ignored a friend who needed you. When you remember these things, you feel guilt and shame. You wish you could correct the damage done, but you don't know how to contact the people. There is a way to deal with such burdens.

In the left column below, list the names of the people you would like to contact. In the right column, briefly describe the situation. When your list is complete, pray through the list one at a time. In prayer, describe what happened and why you feel badly about it. Express your sorrow and guilt. Ask God to forgive you, and help the person you're praying for to understand how sorry you feel. Take as long as you need to "talk it out." Finally, ask God to heal your memory of the pain you've carried with regard to these people.

"Forgive us our sins, just as we have forgiven those who have sinned against us" (Matt. 6:12 NLT).

If you are studying in a small group, discuss this exercise and its purpose, but complete it privately.

Name   Situation

1. _____

_____

2. _____

_____

3. _____

_____

BIBLICAL MANDATE

Scripture has much to say about forgiveness, both in instruction and examples. Taste a sample of God's delicious forgiveness in the passages below:

> And I will forgive their wickedness and will never again remember their sins. (Jer. 31:34 NLT)

> But if we confess our sins to him, he is faithful and just to forgive us and to cleanse us from every wrong. (1 John 1:9 NLT)

> Instead, be kind to each other, tenderhearted, forgiving one another, just as God through Christ has forgiven you. (Eph. 4:32 NLT)

> You must make allowance for each other's faults and forgive the person who offends you. Remember, the Lord forgave you, so you must forgive others. (Col. 3:13 NLT)

We also get biblical examples. For example, Jesus Christ gave His life for the sole purpose of forgiving our sins. His forgiveness was extended to us even before we were aware of the need. It is very clear that He wants us to be forgiving toward everyone we encounter in life. Consider His admonition: "If you forgive those who sin against you, your heavenly Father will forgive you. But if you refuse to forgive others, your Father will not forgive your sins" (Matt. 6:14–15 NLT). What clearer teaching on the necessity of forgiving is there?

Another scriptural example uses math to express the immensity of forgiveness. It is Matthew 18:21–22. In Jesus' story, we are told to forgive seven times seventy times, or 490 times! Think about that. Is 490 the limit of forgiveness? Is that all that is required? Just forgive 490 times, and on the 491st time, we can be unforgiving and hold a grudge? Of course not! Jesus employed hyperbole to make His point. His intent is simple. Forgive 490 times, then another 490, then another; as long as it takes to truly forgive. Do you understand the example? Jesus is telling us to do whatever it takes, as many times as it takes, to ensure that we have forgiven those who harmed us and let go of our grudges.

Following the Civil War, Robert E. Lee went on a tour of the South in an attempt to heal the wounds of the Civil War. He encouraged Southerners to forgive and move on with their lives. At one stop in Georgia, he encountered a lady whose plantation home had been burned by the Union army. In front of her home she had a beautiful old tree, more than one hundred years old. As Lee tried to console the woman, she complained angrily about her tree. She spoke venomously of the Union soldiers. Her personal grudge was deeply entrenched, and her anger was overwhelming. Finally, the lady looked straight into Lee's eyes and demanded, "What should I do, sir?" Lee looked back at her and said, "Cut it down, ma'am, cut it down!"

There comes a time to let go of the grudges and unforgiveness. With God's help, we must "cut them down" and set ourselves free.

A TOOL FOR PRACTICAL FORGIVENESS

As we near the end of chapter 7, you may realize that you need to ask for forgiveness or extend it to others. If you feel that "tug" in your heart, know that it is the Holy Spirit and now is the time to respond.

Reread pages 139–41 in *Healing Is a Choice*. There you will find examples of letters that can be used to ask for, or give, forgiveness. Obviously, the best way to seek or give forgiveness is personally, but there are times when distance, emotions, and circumstances prevent personal contact. These letters provide an option. Review the examples and select one or two that feel comfortable. Use them as often as necessary.

THE SEVENTH BIG LIE:
"Forgiveness is only for those who deserve it or earn it."

By definition, *deserve* means to "be worthy of." The lie states that we are forgiven because we've earned it. It implies that we've done something to suddenly "be worthy of" forgiveness. This simply is not true, never has been, and never will be. No human being merits forgiveness. Scripture reminds us that "all have sinned; all fall short of God's glorious standard" (Rom. 3:23 NLT). "All" means you and me and everyone else!

We don't deserve what God is willing to give us. This is not something we can earn. It is a free gift of grace from a holy and righteous God, who paid an incredible price to arrange for us to have it!

How should we respond? First, we should be receptive of His grace. Second, we must not keep His grace to ourselves. Forgiveness is not a secret. It's the best news in the world!

Remember that God gave us grace we did not deserve or earn. We can do the same. We can give grace to those who have hurt us. They may not deserve it, and by their actions, they may not have earned it. It doesn't matter, because it doesn't depend on them at all. It depends on us. Like God, we can give grace where it is undeserved. We can forgive though no amends have been made. We have the power to set captives free!

Those who have hurt or abused us are in a prison of our creation. We hold the keys to the prison. The keys we hold are anger, grudges, hatred, ill will, and more. We hold those keys in our hands. We want those who have hurt us to come to us begging forgiveness, but they can't. They are consigned to our prison. We have to unlock the door and let them go. By doing that, we no longer have to attend to or feed them. They are no longer our responsibility.

When we set the captives free, we can move forward into the future without having to take them with us. Here is the wonderful resolution. No one deserved this, but now everyone is free! You are free from grudges and anger that hold you in bondage.

They are free, because they are no longer held in the prisons of your mind. "So if the Son sets you free, you will indeed be free" (John 8:36 NLT). And if the Son, Jesus Christ, sets us free, we must also set the captives in our prisons free!

There is a holy irony in this. Forgiveness always bears good fruit. When we set captives free, that act of grace becomes the beginning of healing in people's lives.

In the last section of chapter 7, there is a short story about a deeply wounded lady who had been hurt so badly that forgiveness seemed impossible to her. She was raped at a young age and kept it hidden for years. She suffered physical pain and developed addictive behaviors. Finally, she reached a crisis point and made a courageous healing choice to recover her life. She chose to do three powerful things:

1. She turned to God for comfort. Doing that, she stopped allowing addictions to comfort her any longer. Instead, she found her comfort in God and His unconditional love.

2. She connected with people who could help her. We have thoroughly discussed the importance and value of being connected with others.

3. She sought treatment for her pain. She realized that the only thing more difficult than being healed would be to continue to live unhealed.

As a result of her healing choices, she experienced God's forgiveness at deeper levels than she had ever experienced. She began to tell trusted friends about her past. She gradually overcame her bitterness and resentment. She was released from her bondage.

She stopped viewing herself as a victim. The power of forgiveness radically changed her life.

These three steps will work for all who make the choice to be healed. Will you make that choice? Don't hold grudges; it's bad for your health!

JOURNALING

Take a few minutes and review chapter 7. Every chapter in *Healing Is a Choice* is important, but this chapter speaks to one of the most common of human relational needs, so it is especially valuable. As you write, remember times when you have been hurt and have found forgiveness to be difficult. Remember a time when you needed forgiveness. How did that feel? Did you receive it? Think about forgiveness as you write.

_____

_____

_____

_____

_____

_____

_____

_____

_____

_____

_____

Prayerful Meditation

As is the custom, find a quiet, relaxing place where you are relaxed and uninterrupted. Find a comfortable chair or sofa. Take a few minutes and think about the love of God toward you. Ask the Holy Spirit to give you a genuine understanding and appreciation of forgiveness.

Reflect on the forgiveness quotes listed below. Each one provides a slightly different slant to help us better understand forgiveness. Read each one and think about it for a while. Absorb its meaning into your mind and heart.

Forgiveness is the economy of the heart . . . Forgiveness saves the expense of anger, the cost of hatred, the waste of spirits.

—Hannah More

Any man can seek revenge; it takes a king or a prince to grant a pardon.

—Arthur J. Rehrat

When you forgive, you in no way change the past—but you sure do change the future.

—Bernard Meltzer

When a deep injury is done to us, we never recover until we forgive.

Forgiving isn't forgetting—it's remembering and letting it go.

A good marriage is the union of two forgivers!

I can forgive, but I cannot forget, is only another way of saying, I cannot forgive. Forgiveness ought to be like a canceled note—torn in two and burned up so that it never can be shown against one."

—Henry Ward Beecher

If God were not willing to forgive sin, heaven would be empty.

—German Proverb

Forgiveness is almost a selfish act because of its immense benefits to the one who forgives.

—Josh Billings (1818–1885)

Forgiveness is setting a prisoner free and then discovering the prisoner was you.

Forgiveness is a choice. It is not a feeling, but an act of the will.

—John Eldredge

Don't wait to forgive until you feel like forgiving; you will never get there. Feelings take time to heal after the choice to forgive is made.

—Neil Anderson

It is by forgiving that one is forgiven.

—Mother Teresa

Think about how forgiveness changes your life and gives you hope. Remember that forgiving is a powerful and divine act. God wants you to experience it at its deepest levels. Look deep inside yourself and ask, "How am I doing in terms of forgiving others?" As the Holy Spirit to help you answer that important question.

PRAYER

Forgiving Father, I admit that I have held and nurtured grudges and hard feelings against a number of people. (Name those people, whether living or dead.) Forgiving these people is very hard, but I acknowledge that it is Your will for me to do that. I do forgive them now. I ask You to heal the wounds and painful memories of my life. I cannot make this choice without Your help. Please send Your Holy Spirit to help seal the choice I have made to forgive and heal. Take from my heart and mind any ill feelings, grudges, resentments, and anger. I acknowledge that these feelings are not Your will for my life. Help me to be as forgiving to others as You are to me. In the name of the One who died to forgive my sins. Amen.

8

The Eighth Choice:
The Choice to Risk Your Life

The Eighth Big Lie:
"I must protect myself from any more pain."

"Twenty years from now you will be more disappointed by the things that you didn't do than by the ones you did do. So throw off the bowlines. Sail away from the safe harbor. Catch the trade winds in your sails. Explore. Dream. Discover." Mark Twain wrote those words. Could he be right?

Will we sit down at some point in the future and realize that we missed great opportunities that would have enriched our lives? Will we approach the end of our lives filled with regrets and missed opportunities? From a more positive perspective, how can we live life to its fullest?

One thing is certain. We will never live a full life without being willing to take some risks. Choosing to risk your life is the theme of chapter 8.

Simply reading the opening paragraph may cause you to feel anxious. Risk is hard for you. You don't consider yourself to be brave. You get tense around risk-takers. You panic when someone challenges you to take a risk. Even now, you're thinking, *This is a really good book. Why did it have to be ruined by including this chapter?*

Please don't stop reading. The discussion about risk is not as threatening as you might fear. It is very important and involves another choice to heal. By the way, you won't be asked to sail across the ocean alone, or hang-glide in the Rocky Mountains. Nor will we ask you to do anything reckless.

Before we tackle this important subject, let's look at where we've been:

- In chapter 1, we discussed the critical need to connect with other people who can help and support us in our time of need.

- Chapter 2 encouraged us to really "feel" our lives, instead of denying or running from them. Pain lets us know that we are ill and need to make a choice to heal.

- The next chapter challenged us to investigate our lives. If we are going to make healing choices, we need to identify the places that need correction and improvement.

- Chapter 4 encouraged us to heal our future. The challenge was to acknowledge our losses, grieve them, and make healing choices that propel us into the future.

- Chapter 5 taught us to heal our lives by making the choice to heal. Acknowledging our need to help our lives motivates us to put away the false hope of self-help and consider seeking professionals who can assist us in the healing process.

- Chapter 6 introduced us to the wonderful power of redemption, which changes our lives and gives us hope. It deals with our sins and motivates us to seek the healing we need.

- Chapter 7 introduced one of the most important points in the book, the power of forgiveness, which is the only reliable means to combat the anger, bitterness, and resentment resulting from human failure.

We have come a long way on the journey to be healed. Hopefully, you noticed that each lesson connects with the previous one to strengthen and guide us toward healing.

When we complete the study, you will have vital information necessary to embrace and heal your life. However, the choice is up to you. Healing is a choice. It is God's choice, but you can, and should, join the effort. God wants to heal you. He asks you to participate with Him in that process. Chapter 8 calls you to become boldly involved in the healing effort.

THE EIGHTH CHOICE:
The Choice to Risk Your Life

A POINT OF DECISION

You have reached an important juncture in this study. Now, you are faced with two choices. The first and best choice is to keep making healing choices and move forward. The second choice is to remain where you are. If you take the second choice, you will most likely get "stuck" and miss the opportunity to heal your life.

Why would anyone take the second option? Why bring your life to a halt and never move on?

On the surface, that question sounds absurd. Of course people will choose to move on! But that is not the case. Some decide to stay where they are because they are afraid. The present is familiar to them. Their predictable routines are comfortable and serve as protective walls keeping them sequestered. Within their walls, they are safe and protected from pain. In contrast, the future is unknown and unpredictable. Moving forward feels dangerous. Fear immobilizes them and they get "stuck." Their "protective walls" have infected them with what *Healing Is a Choice* describes as "soul rot."

For these folks, the decision to move ahead reduces to one important personal question, "Am I willing to take risks?"

Everyone must wrestle with the reality of risk, because we cannot live without encountering it.

What is the definition of *risk*? It has two prominent meanings:

- The possibility of suffering harm or loss; danger.
- A factor, thing, element, or course involving uncertain danger.

The definition assumes we will take risks, and it assumes the possibility of some danger. So, we must consider how much risk to take and when it is or is not appropriate.

Exercise #1: How Much Risk Will I Tolerate?

By yourself or in a small group, answer and discuss the following questions.

1. *In your own words, describe what you think the term "soul-rot" means.*

_____

_____

_____

2. *If you are studying in a small group, take a few minutes to share your definitions. Discuss the dangers of "soul-rot."*

_____

_____

_____

3. *How might a person catch the "soul-rot" disease?*

_____

_____

_____

4. *List some ways to combat the dangers of "soul-rot."*

_____

_____

_____

5. *Complete a personal "risk appraisal." Follow these instructions:*

    (a) For each statement below, answer yes or no by checking the appropriate line.

    (b) On the lines below each statement, explain why you answered yes or no.

QUESTIONS   YES   NO

1. *I never take risks!*

_____

_____

2. *I enjoy taking risks, and am a risk-taker by nature.*

_____

_____

3. *I take risks occasionally, only when absolutely necessary.*

_____

_____

4. *I believe it is important to take risks on a regular basis.*

_____

_____

5. *I have often failed when taking risks.*

_____

_____

6. *I have been successful when taking risks.*

_____

_____

When you have completed this exercise, ask a trusted friend to sit with you and discuss your responses. Some thoughtful discussion questions include:

- Do I avoid risks?
- Why am I reluctant to take risks?
- Can I live a full life without any risks?
- Am I harming my life by being reluctant to take risks?
- How can I begin taking some risks that will build my confidence and strength?

RISK IS INEVITABLE!

Some people believe they can avoid taking risks. However, that is not reality. It is magical thinking.

Helen Keller said, "Security is mostly a superstition. It does not exist in nature, nor do the children of men as a whole experience it. Avoiding danger is no safer in the long run than outright exposure. Life is either a daring adventure or nothing."

If anyone was ever entitled to build walls of protection and live in isolation, it was Keller. Yet, her life was one of the most meaningful and important in United States history. Keller took a risk every time she took a step.

Scripture warns us that life is filled with risks. "When you work in a quarry, stones might fall and crush you! When you chop wood, there is danger with each stroke of your ax! Such are the risks of life" (Eccl. 10:9 NLT).

The result of taking no risks is not safety and security. The result of taking no risks is withdrawal, isolation, and even dishonesty.

Why is it dishonest? If you believe you can avoid risks, you are mistaken. No one lives life without risks. It is a lie to believe otherwise. Each of us runs the risk of contracting disease, being hurt by friends, or injuring ourselves. Even if we locked ourselves in a room alone, bolted the doors, and nailed the windows shut, we would still face some risks.

You cannot protect yourself from pain. You are subject to the human condition. By trying to avoid risks, you will harm yourself, becoming disconnected from the friends and family you need. You will become isolated and preoccupied with your safety. You may experience "soul-rot."

The simple truth is that life without risk is not much of a life, or, to take it one step further, "Life without risks is not life at all."

Ouch! Life without risks is not life at all? That is true because life is filled with risks of various kinds. If you are going to live, you will face risks. Life requires it!

BARRIERS TO RISK

Risk has some natural enemies. Two of them are predictability and comfort.

Predictability is like a straitjacket, keeping us wrapped tightly, unable to move about, and stuck in one environment. It prevents us from growing and exploring the wonders of life. Many people put themselves in psychological and emotional straitjackets or predictability. Thus, they are immobilized. To be sure, there is some security that results from things remaining the same. The danger comes from maintaining predictability at the expense of what God wants you to do with your life. His will is not our predictability, but our willingness to join the grand adventure of introducing Jesus Christ to the world!

A second enemy of risk is comfort. It drains the joy out of life. Comfort is a dream killer! There are people who will not join a mission team to a foreign country because they will not have a comfortable bed to sleep on, or a warm shower at the end of the workday. They value comfort more than Christian service. Sadly, they will never experience the utter exhilaration of building a church, running a medical clinic, teaching uneducated children, feeding the hungry, or giving water to the thirsty.

In this matter, we should learn from Jesus, who said,

"Foxes have dens to live in, and birds have nests, but I, the Son of Man, have no home of my own, not even a place to lay my head." He said to another person, "Come, be my disciple." The man agreed, but he said, "Lord, first let me return home and bury my father." Jesus replied, "Let those who are spiritually dead care for their own dead. Your duty is to go and preach the coming of the Kingdom of God." Another said, "Yes, Lord, I will follow you, but first let me say good-bye to my family." But Jesus told him, "Anyone who puts a hand to the plow and then looks back is not fit for the Kingdom of God." (Luke 9:58–62 NLT)

Imagine you live in the early part of the first century AD. You are a disciple of Jesus Christ, who was recently crucified and then, to everyone's amazement, resurrected to life. You follow the risen Christ to Galilee. Now, with some friends, you've gathered on a mountain to hear Him preach. To your surprise, He does not offer a sermon. Instead, He utters four sentences that will change the course of world history.

Listen to Him: "I have been given complete authority in heaven and on earth. Therefore, go and make disciples of all the nations, baptizing them in the name of the Father and the Son and the Holy Spirit. Teach these new disciples to obey all the commands I have given you. And be sure of this: I am with you always, even to the end of the age" (Matt. 28:18–20 NLT).

Think about those precious words. Who would have thought that such brief and beautiful words would contain within them such tremendous risks?

In subsequent years, Jesus' followers took incredible risks for

His sake. They were rejected, repudiated, beaten, whipped, tortured, burned, thrown to animals, hanged, imprisoned, and more. Through the centuries, Christians became acquainted with every known instrument of torture!

Yet, the world today is predominantly Christian due to the fact that a handful of believers were willing to accept the risks in order to obey Christ.

Would anyone suggest that risks taken for Jesus' sake were not worth it? No! Every risk taken to spread the gospel was, and is, worth any consequence.

Yet some people, bound tightly by predictability and comfort, will not risk stepping out of their routines for Jesus' sake!

This chapter calls risk a healing choice. At first that sounds strange, like a contradiction in terms. However, a little thought confirms the truth of the statement. Risk tears the cocoon that binds us right off our bodies. Risk sets us free to be really alive. It forces us to connect with people and experience the thrill of being alive.

If we do not take risks, our lives will be horribly boring and lonely. They will be unexamined lives, devoid of purpose.

Healing Is a Choice teaches that accepting risks is a decision to heal. It forces us to experience life in ways we've never before known. We begin to live as Jesus wants us to, connected to one another; working, growing, and living together for common purposes. Getting to that place may sometimes be painful, but it is well worth it!

Exercise #2: One Man's Example

Turn to chapter 8 in the book and reread pages 151–52 under the heading "Real Risk." Answer the following questions. If you are studying in a small group, discuss the questions aloud.

1. *What was the true risk that Talib Alhamdani faced? Was it returning to a hostile and dangerous environment? Was it the fear of not helping his people? Or, was it what* Healing Is a Choice *states on page 151: "Some people are so afraid of NOT making a difference that risk does not seem much of a factor to them"? Could that have been the motivation that propelled Talib to take such a great risk? Discuss.*

_____

_____

_____

_____

2. *Each of us can make a real difference in some area of life. True or false? How?*

_____

_____

_____

_____

3. *In order to make a difference in life, we must be willing to work through our fears and venture into the world with all its risks. We must accept the reality of risk, and live with it, rather than cowering in fear. Ask yourself, "Can I do that? Am I willing to take some risks to achieve the will of God in my life?"*

_____

_____

_____

_____

4. *Paragraph three on page 152 states: "When you are able to navigate life with a healthy awareness of danger, but willing to take risks to make a difference, you begin to live life in a new dimension." Discuss that statement in your small group, focusing on the twin goals of*
(a) healthy awareness of danger
(b) (being) willing to take risks to make a difference.
Ask and discuss: How do those two goals work together in our lives?

_____

_____

_____

WHAT ARE YOU MISSING?

We must face an important truth. If we choose a predictable and comfortable life without any risks, we will certainly miss many wonderful things.

A very famous poem, most often attributed to poet laureate Alfred Lord Tennyson, says:

> I hold it true, whate'er befall;
> I feel it, when I sorrow most;
> 'Tis better to have loved and lost
> Than never to have loved at all.

His point is simple. It is better to take a risk for a good reason and fail, than never to try. The joy and meaning come to us in the process more than the outcome. It's the endeavor that counts most.

Classical Latin vocabulary includes the word *praxis*. It is the root of our English word *practice*. *Praxis* roughly means "the meaning of something comes in the doing of it." Thus, if you want to be a great tennis player, you must play a lot of tennis. The meaning of tennis to you and how proficient you become are the result of constant practice and improvement. If you want to be a great teacher, you must practice. If you want to be adept at risk-taking, you must practice. You must "experience" some risks in order to manage it well. The good news is, you can do it! "Praxis" makes perfect!

If you are unwilling to take a risk, you may miss a relationship with a fabulous person. You might miss seeing people's lives dramatically changed because you were not part of a mission team. Perhaps the greatest loss will be the opportunity to become the person God planned you to be!

By now, you might be thinking, *I understand. It makes sense, but risk is dangerous. I will get hurt.* The truth is that you may experience some hurt, but the pain of not taking a risk is ultimately greater and more injurious to our psyches than any pain we'd feel in the risk. A wise man once wrote, "A ship in its harbor is safe, but that is not what ships are for!" Ships were meant to sail!

Furthermore, it is important to realize that risk does not mean running headlong into harm's way.

There is a business science called "risk management" that seeks to measure the degree of danger or threat in a given risk. To some extent, we all do some risk management.

Jesus was using risk management at the wedding in Cana in John 2:

The next day Jesus' mother was a guest at a wedding celebration in the village of Cana in Galilee. Jesus and his disciples were also invited to the celebration. The wine supply ran out during the festivities, so Jesus' mother spoke to him about the problem. "They have no more wine," she told him. "How does that concern you and me?" Jesus asked. "My time has not yet come." (vv. 1–4 NLT)

Jesus' mother asked Him to solve an embarrassing situation. To do it required a miracle. Jesus weighed the risk. If He performed the miracle, word would quickly spread and a confrontation with His enemies might occur before He was ready to reveal Himself publicly. That is what Jesus meant when He said, "My time has not yet come." Still, He considered His mother's request, and He cared about the wedding and guests. Ultimately, He weighed the risk and performed the miracle.

We must all do some risk management. Some people will take greater risks than others. That is natural. What is not natural is to take no risks. All people need to take some risks at some time. Risks are necessary to live a full life. It may even be painful at times, but it is the pain that lets you know you are alive!

Life without any risks is no life at all! It's existence, but it's not life!

PICK A BUDDY

One way to manage risk is to employ a "buddy system." Some people never take risks, because of pain and injury sustained early in life. They cannot envision taking a risk of any kind, especially alone. However, with a friend, they might be persuaded. With a buddy, there is enough security to take a risk or two.

Jesus understood that principle and dispatched His disciples in a buddy system. "And he called his twelve disciples together and sent them out two by two, with authority to cast out evil spirits" (Mark 6:7 NLT).

The buddy system has worked for centuries throughout the world and is an effective way to turn a risk-avoider into a risk-taker.

Consider selecting a "buddy." Is there a person or two in your life who could become a buddy and help you learn to take some risks? Think carefully about this choice.

1. List several potential buddies on the lines below in order of your preference.

_____

_____

_____

2. Contact the first person on your list. Explain that you want to be a bit bolder and take a few risks (nothing dramatic, just small steps). Ask the person to join you for support and fellowship. Give them permission to push you a bit. Pick a challenge together. Be sure it is manageable, but also be sure there is some degree of risk involved. When you conquer your first challenge, move ahead to a new one and conquer it, too! Ask your buddy how you're doing. Accept his or her encouragement and support. Together, you can conquer your fear and build a track record of success and confidence. Your life will change! You will feel the confidence build inside. You will feel an urge to do more.

3. If your first selection for a buddy does not work out, contact the second person on your list and try again. Above all, do not give up. Push through your fear. Throw away the "ways that you are set in."

Exercise 3: The Courage to Take Risks

Ralph Waldo Emerson wrote, "Whatever you do, you need courage. Whatever course you set, there is always someone to tell you that you are wrong. There are always difficulties arising that tempt you to believe your critics are right. To map out a course of action and follow it to an end requires some of the same courage that a soldier needs. Peace has its victories, but it takes brave men and women to win them."

Perhaps it's been a while since you've taken a risk. Here is an exercise to use as you venture into the world of "risk-taking." None of these things are threatening or dangerous, but doing them will build your confidence. Completing them in sequence will make it easier. It will take some time to accomplish these things. Don't be pressured by time, but don't put them off. Doing them will help you become comfortable with risks and will invest you in self-improvement and the Lord's work.

Check each one as you complete it.
1. _____ Phone a friend you haven't heard from in a while and get reacquainted.
2. _____ If you haven't been out of your house or apartment for a while, go to lunch at a new restaurant, or go see a movie.

3. _____ Call your church and volunteer to help with an outreach ministry such as inner-city feeding, a homeless shelter, or literacy program.

4. _____ Bake cookies or a casserole and take it to your neighbor. If invited, stay and visit for a while.

5. _____ Invite a friend or a relative to an amusement park. Ride a roller coaster.

6. _____ Call your pastor and ask if you can share your testimony in a midweek service, small group, or Sunday school class. Prior to sharing, write your testimony and rehearse it several times, so you will be comfortable and natural as you tell your story.

7. _____ Join a team that provides worship services for senior citizens. Involve yourself in the worship.

8. _____ Contact someone with whom you have been estranged. Make a committed effort to reconcile with that person.

9. _____ Join a small group at your church and faithfully attend the meetings. Get to know the other participants. Get involved in the Bible studies and sharing.

10. _____ Plan a mini-vacation out of town. Visit a location you've long wanted to see. Create an itinerary, make housing reservations, have your car serviced, and enjoy yourself.

Each time you accomplish one of the risk-challenges listed above, you will grow stronger and more confident. You will feel energy gathering inside you.

Taking risks requires courage. That point is made vividly in Frank Baum's story *The Wonderful Wizard of Oz.*[1] Most people have read the book or seen the 1939 movie. It's a great story about taking risks. Dorothy was caught in a storm and mysteriously arrived in the land of Oz. Her only way home was to move forward and find the Wizard of Oz, who supposedly had the power to transport her home. Along the journey to Oz, Dorothy made three friends, all struggling with their own weaknesses and liabilities. They were a tinman, a strawman, and a cowardly lion. Each was afraid and embarrassed by his own deficiency. Like Dorothy, they needed to take the risk of finding Oz. The journey was long and dangerous. They forced themselves to move forward, battling and overcoming, always staying on the yellow brick road. The journey to Oz changed each of them. When they finally arrived at Oz, they were shocked. The powerful Wizard of Oz was no wizard at all. Rather, he was a mere mortal. He was incapable of performing the magic that would send Dorothy home, give the lion a heart, put a brain in the Strawman or place a heart in the Tinman.

But wait! They suddenly realized that the journey had changed each of them. Dorothy found her way home. Suddenly, the lion was courageous. The Tinman felt emotions. The Strawman was smart.

The Wizard of Oz is a story about risk, growth, and maturity. Each character began the journey handicapped. Dorothy was lost and displaced. The lion was bound by fear. The Strawman suffered from the bondage of inferiority. The Tinman had lost touch with his feelings.

Yet, they all realized that their only hope was to move ahead. They had no real choice but to take the risks.

Notice the important fact that they took the journey together. They connected with one another and found mutual support and, ultimately, love. Each of them mustered up what little courage they could find, headed down the yellow brick road as a team, and completed their quest confident and strong.

The Wizard of Oz is a metaphor for everyone who is immobilized and unwilling to take risks.

Here is a simple fact of life: We all must take risks in life. They are inevitable. The worst that can happen is that we might fail, but if we do, God is there with us, loving, nudging, and pushing us to try again. His love allows us to move beyond our fears. Taking a risk to move boldly into the future is a healing choice, and a prelude to leaving the past behind.

"One does not discover new lands without consenting to lose sight of the shore for a very long time" (Andre Gide, twentieth-century French writer, 1947 Nobel Prize winner).

Scripture reminds us that God's "love has no fear because perfect love expels all fear. If we are afraid, it is for fear of judgment, and this shows that his love has not been perfected in us" (1 John 4:18 NLT).

"For God has not given us a spirit of fear and timidity, but of power, love, and self-discipline" (2 Tim. 1:7 NLT).

Healing Is a Choice makes an emphatic point: "If you are living in fear, you are not living as God intended; He wants you free from fear."

THE EIGHTH BIG LIE:

"I must protect myself from any more pain."

We called chapter 6's big lie a "whopper"! This chapter's lie is the Mt. Everest of lies! People are not capable of protecting themselves from pain.

Trying to protect yourself from pain only makes your life more miserable. If you are in a defensive mode, you will be preoccupied with pain. You will worry about your body. You will probably develop psychosomatic symptoms because you are so worried.

Anxiety and fear will grow stronger in you.

At some time in your life you are going to be hurt, and there's nothing you can do about it. That's life. It will probably happen more than once. However, you can be sure that Jesus will never leave or forsake you. You can be fortified by that truth and draw strength from it.

As repeated a number of times in *Healing Is a Choice*, you must make a decision to be healed. Healing is God's choice, but we must cooperate with Him and not resist what He is doing in our lives. The choice to heal by taking risks is one of the most powerful decisions you will make. Be not afraid! It was Will Rogers who said, "Don't be afraid to go out on a limb. That's where the fruit is."

JOURNALING

The book reminds us that risk is a healer. Risk demands faith and trust. It forbids us from living a life of self-preservation. Are you ready to take some risks? What are the things that continue to stand in your way, blocking your path?

Remember that the powerful Holy Spirit is standing with you. He is your champion, and you can draw courage and strength from Him. This is the day to put away all the old, stifling patterns of your life. This is the day that all things become new! Spend time processing these thoughts and record your feelings as you journal.

_____

_____

_____
_____
_____
_____
_____
_____
_____
_____
_____
_____
_____

PRAYERFUL MEDITATION

Chapter 8 asks us to meditate on Deuteronomy 31:6, "Be strong and courageous! Do not be afraid of them! The LORD your God will go ahead of you. He will neither fail you nor forsake you" (NLT).

You will find these words on page 162, "God will never forsake you. There is nothing you can do to run God off. He will never leave you. He will always be there for you. God created you and will always be there for you. If God is for you in that way, who could possibly be against you? God loves you. He is there for you and you need have no fear of today or what tomorrow may bring."

PRAYER

God of Power and Might, I confess my fears and my reluctance to take risks. I've become very familiar with the ruts in *which I live. The truth is that they are very uncomfortable and constricting. I often dream of reaching out, being brave and bold. I am ready for change. Please help me. Help me risk connecting, so I don't die in isolation. Help me risk loving again, so I won't become bitter and isolated. Help me risk succeeding, knowing I could fail. Spare me from a horrible life of boredom and loneliness. Send Your Holy Spirit to give me courage. Help me not to be dissuaded. Block me from retreating back into my ruts. I want my life to count for You and for me. Heal my fear. Give me strength today to make the healing choice to take some risks for Your kingdom's sake, through Christ, my Champion, amen.*

9

THE NINTH CHOICE:
The Choice to Serve

THE NINTH BIG LIE:
"Until I am completely healed and strong, there is no place for me to serve God."

He appeared at the door of the plane, saluted smartly, then made his way carefully down the steep steps. Stopping in front of the microphone, his rugged face haggard, yet calm, he said, "We are honored to have served our country under difficult circumstances." America watched, moved by the sight of this man just released from years of captivity in North Vietnam, as he expressed his gratitude and ended unforgettably with, "God bless America!"

The man was Captain Jeremiah Denton. The date was February 11, 1973.

Those words, "We are honored . . . ," have clung hauntingly to my mind down through the years. They were underscored in February ten years later, when the film clip was again aired on national television accompanied in person by Jeremiah Denton, then a U.S. senator.

All this is a prelude to one thought: Is this how the believer will feel when he stands one day before God? Liberated from this earth and its struggles, will we say, "We are honored to have served . . . under difficult circumstances"?[1]

Have you had an opportunity to say that? Has there been a time in your life when you were able to serve God, even under difficult circumstances? Or, are you still waiting for an opportunity?

THE NINTH CHOICE:
The Choice to Serve

Judges 6 records the story of God offering Gideon the opportunity for meaningful service:

> Then the angel of the LORD came and sat beneath the oak tree at Ophrah, which belonged to Joash of the clan of Abiezer. Gideon son of Joash had been threshing wheat at the bottom of a winepress to hide the grain from the Midianites. The angel of the LORD appeared to him and said, "Mighty hero, the LORD is with you!" "Sir," Gideon replied, "if the LORD is with us, why has all this happened to us? And where are all the miracles our ancestors told us about? Didn't they say, 'The LORD brought us up out of Egypt?' But now the LORD has abandoned us and handed us over to the Midianites." Then the LORD turned to him and said, "Go with the strength you have and rescue Israel from the Midianites. I am sending you!" "But Lord," Gideon replied, "how can I rescue Israel? My clan is the weakest in the whole tribe of Manasseh, and I am the least in my entire family!" The LORD said to him, "I will be with you. And you will destroy the Midianites as if you were fighting against one man." (vv. 11–16, NLT)

Gideon was skeptical, a tough sell! He had heard many accounts of the wonderful things God had done for Israel in the past, but had not seen anything like that in his lifetime. Further, he pointed out that his tribe, Manasseh, was the weakest clan in Israel, and among them, he was the weakest person.

Gideon felt insecure and unprepared, the weakest member of a weak family. He was the most unlikely candidate to be commander in chief of the Israeli army. However, it didn't matter, because God was with him and Gideon did lead Israel to victory against the Midianites.

Just as God was with Gideon, He is with us. You may not feel qualified. Neither did Gideon. You may feel weak and inadequate. So did Gideon. You may feel you have no apparent skills or qualifications. That's just how Gideon felt. You might say to yourself, "I am not wise. I don't know where or how to begin." Listen to what God says to that:

This "foolish" plan of God is far wiser than the wisest of human plans, and God's weakness is far stronger than the greatest of human strength. Remember, dear brothers and sisters, that few of you were wise in the world's eyes, or powerful, or wealthy when God called you. Instead, God deliberately chose things the world considers foolish in order to shame those who think they are wise. And he chose those who are powerless to shame those who are powerful. God chose things despised by the world, things counted as nothing at all, and used them to bring to nothing what the world considers important, so that no one can ever boast in the presence of God. God alone made it possible for you to be in Christ Jesus. For our benefit God made Christ to be wisdom itself. He is the one who made us acceptable to God. He made us pure and holy, and he gave himself to purchase our freedom. As the Scriptures say, "The person who wishes to boast should boast only of what the Lord has done." (1 Cor. 1:25–31 NLT)

GOD IS CALLING YOU INTO SERVICE

The person who feels most inadequate and unprepared is often the one God uses. That teaching is prominent throughout Scripture, yet people will argue every day that they are not capable, worthy, or prepared to serve the kingdom of God. Who is right, God or us? God is right, of course! His track record proves it! He consistently chooses the least likely people to do the most incredible things. The good news is that you can be one of them!

We should not resist God's call into service. Rather, we should be thrilled that He has chosen to use us. In fact, Romans 12:1–2 infers that God would love for us to volunteer rather than wait to be drafted:

And so, dear Christian friends, I plead with you to give your bodies to God. Let them be a living and holy sacrifice—the kind he will accept. When you think of what he has done for you, is this too much to ask? Don't copy the behavior and customs of this world, but let God transform you into a new person by changing the way you think. Then you will know what God wants you to do, and you will know how good and pleasing and perfect his will really is. (NLT)

Our daily prayer should be, Lord, how may I serve You?

What's Your Excuse?

1. *What prevents you from serving? Circle any of the things listed below that keep you from serving. Use the lines at the end of the list to write in things not listed.*

Family demands	Work responsibilities	Financial concerns
Feel unworthy	Illness / health	Feel inadequate
Don't know people	Don't know what to do	No available time
Too shy to volunteer	Embarrassed	Not talented
Not spiritual enough	Not connected to church	No commitment

_____

_____

_____

_____

_____

2. *Working Through the Process*

    (a) *List the five most serious objections from your list on the left line below.*

    (b) *In the spaces to the right, list 3 ways you can overcome your objections.*

#1 _____   _____

#2 _____   _____

#3 _____   _____

#4 _____   _____

#5 _____   _____

3. *Having completed the exercise, ask this important question. Is there a good reason not to offer yourself for service in God's work? Are you holding on to excuses to keep from serving?*

The decision to serve is not so much about your feelings (i.e., "Do you feel like serving or not?"). Rather, it is a very objective decision. This may sound irreligious, but the decision to serve does not require hours of prayer. Why? The answer is simple. Scripture is very forthright about the expectation of serving. Paul reminds us that God created us to serve, specifically to do the good things He planned for us before we were born. Our prayers should be directed toward where, when, and how we will serve, but never "if" we will serve.

"God saved you by his special favor when you believed. And you can't take credit for this; it is a gift from God. Salvation is not a reward for the good things we have done, so none of us can boast about it. For we are God's masterpiece. He has created us anew in Christ Jesus, so that we can do the good things he planned for us long ago" (Eph. 2:8–10 NLT).

Hopefully, these exercises have made an impact on you. Serving is not an option. It is an integral part of a believer's life, as much a part of our lives as the blood that flows through our veins. Serving is not a choice to be made. Rather, it is a manifestation of what it means to be alive.

Jesus said, "For even I, the Son of Man, came here not to be served but to serve others, and to give my life as a ransom for many" (Mark 10:45 NLT).

Jesus came to serve, and we are supposed to be like Him, so we must serve!

COME ALIVE!

When you make the decision to serve, you experience a brand-new way of life. You come alive as never before. One of the most important benefits of serving is that your life suddenly has meaning. In serving, you develop a sense of purpose, a reason for being. As a result, you feel purposeful and motivated. It excites your life!

Typically, when people join a foreign or home mission trip, they change. Perhaps they've built a church or a school. Maybe they've helped run a medical clinic. Whatever the mission, the payoff comes at the end as team members reflect in awe and say things like, "Did I really help do this?" "What a miracle!" or "I would never have imagined I could be part of something like this!" The feeling of having accomplished something remarkable for others is overwhelming.

Richard Foster expresses that feeling in his book *Celebration of Discipline*. He writes, "When we set out on a consciously chosen course of action that accents the good of others and is for the most part a hidden work, a deep change occurs in our spirit."[2]

When people give themselves in service to the kingdom of God, they acquire a deep sense of knowing they are dong exactly what Jesus asked them to do. They find themselves in the very center of God's will. In that moment of realization, they discover who they have truly become.

Like Jesus, we are not on this planet to be served, but to pour our lives out in service to others.

GIVING BACK

The healing choice to serve is one of the most impacting decisions you will ever make. The previous healing choices you've made all combine for this moment when you give yourself back to others, so that they also can make healing choices.

1. *The notion of giving back is based on the premise that God has blessed us, so that we can become conduits through whom He can bless others.*

   (a) To reinforce this point, do the following exercise.

   (b) Read the two passages below. After each, paraphrase the verse using your own words and thoughts.
   "He comforts us in all our troubles so that we can comfort others. When others are troubled, we will be able to give them the same comfort God has given us" (2 Cor. 1:4 NLT).

   _____

   _____

   _____

   _____

"Much is required from those to whom much is given, and much more is required from those to whom much more is given" (Luke 12:48 NLT).

   _____

   _____

   _____

   _____

2. *In your own words, and as fully as you can, describe what the above texts mean to you.*

_____

_____

_____

_____

Here is an important caveat. It may be that you do not feel sufficiently healed to be serving. You may be thinking, *I'm not ready yet,* or *I'm still battling with choices I need to make or lies I need to overcome.* Be very careful. You could hold on to that argument forever and never make any progress.

The fact is that we all are in process. We can serve, though we are still wounded.

Henri Nouwen wrote a book titled *The Wounded Healer.*[3] His premise was that we all could help one another in the healing process, just as we are, wounded and broken. Nouwen said that in order to help those who are suffering, the helper must first recognize his own pain. It is the servant's personal pain that allows him or her to empathize with other needy people to genuinely help them heal.

If you had no pain of your own, how could you understand the pain of others?

Remember that chapter 8 introduced us to the Latin word *praxis.* Praxis teaches us that the meaning of things comes in the doing of them.

It is as you are serving that you become a servant. You don't have to be ever preparing to become a servant. If that were true, most of us would never serve. You can serve as a wounded person who becomes a wounded healer! Gideon overcame his weaknesses. So can you.

Remember the truth in the previous exercise. God comforts us in our troubles so that we can comfort others. Healing is a choice.

The decision to begin serving, even while working through personal issues and struggles, is a healing choice. Yes, you may still be working through pain and grief. You may be working hard to investigate your life and make corrections. You may be experiencing redemption for the first time or working very hard on forgiveness.

Here is an interesting irony. The fact that you are still struggling with issues does not disqualify you from service. Rather, it empowers you. You can draw from the help God's Holy Spirit is giving you in order to help others.

If you were abused or hurt and have begun to recover from those scars, you can use what you have learned about surviving and overcoming to help others. You can empathize with their pain. You know what they are thinking and how it impacts their lives.

Be encouraged! Jump into the healing struggle. Take what is a noble title and use it; you can be a wounded healer as you serve others.

GOD GIVES YOU SECRET POWER!

We have been discussing the fact that God wants you to serve, even though you may still feel wounded and inadequate. We reinforced the idea that He can use you when you are still struggling and wounded. You can be a wounded healer.

However, you might wonder where the strength comes from to serve, even while you are still struggling with issues and pain.

The answer is what *Healing Is a Choice* calls "Secret Powers." Secret powers are supernatural strengths and gifts that God's Holy Spirit gives us to help us serve. God gives gifts to all His children. He personally selects the gifts you receive.

Scripture teaches us that the Holy Spirit disburses a variety of spiritual gifts among believers. Most relevant to our discussion are two categories of gifts mentioned in 1 Corinthians 12:4, 9.

Paul wrote that there are "different kinds of service," and "gifts of healing."

Clearly, God gives us the ability to serve, and in a wide variety of venues and opportunities. In a sense, He individualizes our service. By creating so many service opportunities in the world, we can move toward those that best suit our gifts, talents, and skills. So, serving God can occur in a limitless way. Wherever people need help, believers can respond.

In addition, God gives "gifts of healing." Aren't you glad? Isn't it encouraging to know that healing is available from the One Scripture addresses as the "Great Physician"?

Here are two important truths to understand. First, the fact that God gives "gifts of healing" implies that there is much sickness and pain in the world. Clearly, we wouldn't need healing if everyone was well.

Second, Scripture teaches that God's response to illness and pain is to give us a wide variety of healing options.

At times, we may need medical science to help us heal. God gives doctors and nurses great knowledge and skill to perform their tasks. He gives physicians some of His "gifts of healing."

At other times, we don't need doctors or medication as much as we need love and support. In those situations, God gives other "gifts of healings," which are expressed in human kindness and understanding, support and encouragement.

Spiritual gifts come from God, thus they are, indeed, secret powers. Human beings don't always know how God's gifts of healing work, but there are people who benefit from them every day.

What Is Your Secret Power?

Healing Is a Choice offers ten guiding questions to get you started on the path toward discovering your secret powers. Answering the survey questions will point you in the direction of your spiritual gifts. This exercise asks you to do three things. It will take a while and require some Bible study. Please take time to complete the exercise. What you will discover about yourself may change your life forever and ignite your service with the Holy Spirit's power. Before you start, offer this prayer:

> *Father of all good gifts, thank You for guiding me to this exercise. I realize Your Holy Spirit is speaking to me through this process, so I open my heart and mind to hear. As I read and think and make discoveries in the next few minutes, make Your will clear to me. I know I am not perfect, but I am in the process of growing, thanks to You. I truly want to be a faithful servant, so please speak to me in this exercise. My life belongs to You, Lord. Use it as You have planned. Trusting Christ, who orders my steps, amen.*

Instructions:

1. *Familiarize yourself with biblical texts related to spiritual gifts by reading the passages listed. After each passage, list the spiritual gifts mentioned in the passage. Note gifts that are mentioned more than once.*

   (a) Romans 12:1–8

(b) Ephesians 4:11–13

_____

(c) 1 Peter 4:9–11

_____

(d) 1 Corinthians 12:7–10

_____

2. Read the passages listed below. In the space provided, describe in your own words how they relate to spiritual gifts.

_____

(a) 1 Corinthians 12:4–6

_____

(b) 1 Corinthians 12:11

_____

3. What is the purpose of spiritual gifts? To answer this question, refer to the passages listed below. Then describe the stated purpose of spiritual gifts mentioned in each text.

(a) Romans 12:5

_____

(b) 1 Corinthians 12:7

_____

(c) 1 Corinthians 12:18

_____

(d) 1 Corinthians 12:20–27

_____

(e) 1 Peter 4:10

_____

4. *Respond to each of the ten questions mentioned in chapter 9 under the heading "Survey Yourself." Use a piece of paper to record your responses, or write them in the margin next to each question.*

5. *When you have completed the exercise, take a few minutes to think about what you have read and studied. Think about the ten questions you answered. Based on that, write the spiritual gifts you believe you have in the spaces below.*

_____

_____

_____

_____

6. *There are four ways in which you can test your results.*

   (a) Ask a close Christian friend to respond to your gifts. Do they see those gifts in you? Can they confirm that the gift is working in you?

(b) Schedule an appointment with your pastor. Explain the process you've been through as you've explored spiritual gifts. Ask him to confirm that the gifts identified are working in you.

(c) Is it clear to you that the gifts you identified are being expressed in your life?

(d) Spend time in focused prayer, asking God to either confirm the gifts you've identified or lead you to the correct ones.

This important exercise will get you started on the road to identifying your gifts.

Being aware of your gifts is crucial as you serve, because the gifts given to you by the Holy Spirit are the ones God wants you to use as you serve. You may be surprised to discover that as you serve others, you are experiencing more healing in your own life.

Healing Is a Choice reminds us that making decisions to help others also heals us. The powerful choice to serve does a remarkable thing. It immediately changes your focus. Alone and unconnected to people, we become quickly self-absorbed. Our problems are always on our minds. Our focus on pain makes it more acute. Our loneliness makes us sour and selfish. Thus, our illness becomes worse.

However, the moment we make a healing choice to serve, our entire perspective changes from ourselves to others. Connected to people, we feel less alone. Our problems diminish as we focus on the trouble others are enduring. We feel less personal pain as we focus on relieving the pain of others. Our loneliness diminishes as we encourage and make ourselves available to others. Thus, our pain improves.

When you serve, you bring far more to the effort than you realize. You have your experience. You have the wisdom you have gained as you walked through your own struggles. You have solutions you learned in the "school of hard knocks" that others have not yet experienced. You have victories, great and small, that others are desperately hoping to experience. Will you help those who need you? Will you offer yourself in service? You may be the only person some people will hear. Yours may be the only perspective they see as related to them. You may be their only help!

THE NINTH BIG LIE:
"Until I am completely healed and strong,
there is no place for me to serve God."

Scripture makes it very plain that God uses broken and damaged people before they are healed. In fact, Scripture assumes our brokenness and struggles. To some extent we are all strugglers in this world, experiencing failures more than we'd prefer.

Actually, Scripture is filled with examples of God's good people who experienced huge failures. For example, Cain murdered his brother. Rebekah and Jacob conspired against Isaac and Esau to swindle an inheritance. Moses smote the rock. Eli was a terrible father whose children brought a reproach on the nation. Saul turned into a ruthless despot. David lied to God on three separate occasions. Those lies were so serious that the entire nation of Israel suffered thousands of deaths as a consequence.

Many of Israel's kings led the people into idolatry more than toward God. Prophets sometimes prophesied contrary to God's will, because they were afraid for their lives. Elijah endured a deep, dark depression, because the queen had threatened his life. When God called Jonah to go to Nineveh, he went in exactly the opposite direction. Even after he finally did what God called him to do, he griped and complained.

Peter betrayed Christ. John Mark was such a problem for Barnabas that he was sent home. These are just a few examples.

The Bible is clear about the failures of its characters. It does not withhold the truth.

The irony is that many of the "failures" mentioned above were powerfully used by God to do great things. These were people filled with human foibles, yet God used them. Few of them were completely perfect or healed of their problems when God used them.

The ninth lie is particularly dangerous, because it holds out an impossible expectation and forever leaves people under God's judgment rather than His grace.

Let me explain. The impossible expectation is that I can be completely healed and strong.

It will never happen. As long as we are encumbered in human flesh, we will be susceptible to failure, defeat, illness, and human problems. As long as we are human beings, we will struggle with our pain, disconnectedness, fear of investigating our lives, and unwillingness to serve.

The good news is, God uses fallible humans. It is fortunate that He doesn't use just "completely healed and strong" people, because there would not be any at His disposal. We can be thankful He uses people like us.

The ninth lie holds people under God's judgment because it says, "There is no place for me to serve God." Please understand that God is not placing these folks under His judgment. No, it's the people themselves who have placed themselves under His judgment. God has not condemned them. They have condemned themselves ("There is no place for ME to serve . . ."). The individual has decided he or she cannot serve.

This lie is particularly destructive. It kills hope. It alienates people from God. If we tolerate this dangerous lie, we function in outright contradiction to the will of God.

Here is the good news. You can serve God now, with your faults, failures, weaknesses, pains, and problems. Despite all that and more, God can use you. He takes broken people and enables them to do great things. He takes people's pain and turns it into a positive, productive force.

As *Healing Is a Choice* reminds us, there is a time to serve. No one should serve before they are able. If you are deeply addicted and have relapsed repeatedly, it might not be the time to serve.

On the other hand, no one should wait too long to serve. As soon as you feel some ego-strength, do something for God's sake. You may not be ready to teach Sunday school, but you could mow the church lawn or drive someone to a doctor's appointment.

Serving is a path to healing, so the longer we put off serving, the slower we will heal.

Matthew 25 teaches us that God expects people to use their talents and abilities for His sake. Those who have more talents and abilities have more responsibility. Those with fewer talents must use what they have. Our acts of service mean something important to Christ. They must also mean something important to us.

When we share our lives with others, we are serving Jesus Christ. As a result, when we serve others, God provides more healing for our growth and development, so that we can serve more people, and receive more healing, and serve more until He comes!

JOURNALING

What is the degree and quality of my service for Christ? Am I serving? Is my life making a difference for Jesus' sake? Do I know what my spiritual gifts are? Am I cultivating them for God's purposes on earth? Do I want to be useful in the kingdom of God? These are guiding questions as you begin journaling in response to chapter 9. Take some time to think about the questions and record your thoughts below.

_____

_____

_____

_____

_____

_____

_____

_____

_____

_____

_____

_____

_____

_____

_____

_____

PRAYERFUL MEDITATION

"I have given you an example to follow. Do as I have done to you. How true it is that a servant is not greater than the master. Nor are messengers more important than the one who sends them. You know these things—now do them! That is the path of blessing" (John 13:15–17 NLT).

Think about this text. Are you following Jesus' example of servanthood? Is there any reason why you are not? If so, pray about it. Jesus didn't leave us any choice in the matter. He emphatically called us to serve. Therefore, we must get ourselves into the service mode, active and impacting. At the end of the passage, Jesus said, "That is the path of blessing." The Greek word for blessed, *makarios*, roughly means deep spiritual meaning and fulfillment. Isn't that what we all crave? It can be ours if we will serve.

Clearly, the road to deep meaning and spiritual fulfillment is serving.

PRAYER

Merciful, loving Father, I confess my reluctance to serve. Often, I'm consumed with my own needs and desires. I'm battling my own pain and failures. It's hard for me to believe I can serve anyone in a way that would help him or her. However, I do believe that through Your power and guidance, I can do all things. But I need Your help so much! I don't know where to begin or what to do. Please direct me in the right direction. Today, in this moment of prayer, I give my life to You as a humble servant. Order my steps and guide my efforts. Take me to the people and places where I am most needed. I'm not sure where all this is going, but I absolutely trust You to be with me. Through Christ, my strength, amen.

IO

The Tenth Choice:
The Choice to Persevere

The Tenth Big Lie:
"There is no hope for me."

Dr. Norman Vincent Peale, in a sermon titled "Problems Are Good for You," told the following story.

A young woman stood before a crowd of thousands, watching in disbelief as Queen Elizabeth II approached to crown her the tennis champion of the world. It all seemed so unreal.

The young lady was born to a poor family. She lived on a ramshackle farm outside New York City, and was very ill most of her early years. Her family survived on welfare. She had trouble in school and frequently ran away from home.

"But she had a persevering mother," said Peale, "who one day said to her, 'There's a stone down by the barn. Can you see it, dear?' Peering from the porch, the child recognized the potato-shaped stone. 'I want you to go down there,' her mother went on, 'and bring that stone up here so we can use it as a step by the kitchen door.'"

Sobbing, the child protested, "Mommy, I'm so weak I can hardly walk down there. I can't move the stone alone!" But her mother persevered. "You go down there, child, and if necessary, move it only half an inch at a time, but move it."

Inch by inch over the following days, the little girl did as she was asked, often with tears. It took her two months to do what normally healthy children her age could have done in fifteen minutes. But as she struggled with that stone, she lost her weakness and grew stronger. A few years later she took up tennis. It was a natural fit for her and she began winning tournaments. In time, she became a professional and played her way to the Wimbledon tennis courts, where in 1957, she became the first African-American woman to win both the singles and doubles championships there.

When she returned home to New York City, a ticker-tape parade was held in her honor. The once weak and troubled little girl was applauded by thousands of people standing on the streets to see her, Althea Gibson, one of the greatest tennis players of all time.[1]

Through perseverance and determination, she overcame a poor family environment, bad health, welfare, and prejudice. Her story is a testimony to the incredible power of perseverance.

THE TENTH CHOICE:
The Choice to Persevere

Wait. Be patient. Give it time. Persevere. These are words that frustrate more than encourage us. We live in a culture where things are expected to happen quickly. We want quick food, quick service, and quick healing.

Healing is a choice. It is God's choice. He chooses when and how quickly we will be healed. That fact flies in the face of our impatience. More than anything, we want God to heal us now. We think, *If He would heal me right now, my pain would stop, and that would prove how much He cares for me. Others can have progressive healing; I want a miracle!*

Miracles are by definition rare, yet they do happen. We have every right to pray for miracles, but we must remember they are not the norm. Therefore, most people who suffer are not going to be healed miraculously. They may need medical treatment, medications, counseling, even hospitalization. It may require time and effort for them to be well. If the illness is chronic, they need to have a very large dose of perseverance.

THE TOUGHEST CHOICE

Perseverance is extraordinarily difficult to manage. It doesn't heal us. It just says, "Hang on," "Wait," and "Be patient." Persevering often feels as if nothing positive is happening. That's frustrating, because we crave instant healing.

We feel stuck in our illness. We're still not connected to others. We're grieving and still having trouble forgiving people.

But God is in the persevering. He is doing a healing work. We cannot heal ourselves, but we can make the healing choice to cooperate with God as He heals us. He asks us to have faith and not give up while healing is occurring.

Persevering is tough, but it is also beneficial. You may not enjoy the process, but it produces good fruit in our lives.

We wish we could avoid perseverance. But something marvelous happens to us during the process.

1. *Read the text below:*

   We can rejoice, too, when we run into problems and trials, for we know that they are good for us—they help us learn to endure. And endurance develops strength of character in us, and character strengthens our confident expectation of salvation. (Rom. 5:3–4 NLT)

2. *Paraphrase the text in your own words.*

_____

_____

_____

_____

_____

_____

_____

_____

_____

_____

3. *If you are studying in a small group, discuss your individual paraphrases together.*

4. *According to the verse above, what are the positive benefits of persevering?*

_____

_____

_____

You can see that persevering is an important healing choice.

THE VALUE OF OUR LIVES TO GOD

You may think that your life is not worth much. Your self-esteem was damaged long ago and has not yet been rebuilt. You are persevering, but it's difficult to see any progress. You're tempted to think God has abandoned you.

It's important to remember that your feelings can tell you a direct lie. Human feelings are both fickle and very subjective, causing you to feel great one day and depressed the next. If you live each day based on how you feel, you may crash.

Feelings do not define you, nor should you allow them to control your life. What is necessary is to live life based on God's truth. What is God's truth about you?

Let's explore that.

1. *We know God loves us and values our lives, but to what extent? Find Psalm 139:1–24 in your Bible and read it carefully. You may want to read it several times.*

2. *Identify the "key statements" in the chapter. These statements tell us something about how God relates to us.*

3. *Read the "key statements" below taken from Psalm 139. Think about each one. Meditate on its meaning for a few moments.*

"You know everything about me."
"You know my every thought when far away."
"Every moment you know where I am."

"You know what I am going to say even before I say it."

"You place your hand of blessing on my head."

"I can never escape from your spirit!"

"Your strength will support me."

"You made all the delicate, inner parts of my body."

"Thank you for making me so wonderfully complex!"

"Your workmanship is marvelous."

"You watched me as I was being formed."

"Every day of my life was recorded in your book."

"How precious are your thoughts about me, O God."

"When I wake up in the morning, you are still with me."

"Search me, O God, and know my heart; test me and know my thoughts."

"Point out anything in me that offends you, and lead me along the path of everlasting life."

4. *In the spaces below, describe in your own words how these "key statements" speak to you about your value to God.*

_____

_____

_____

_____

5. *Take some time to offer a prayer of thanksgiving for the astonishing love and commitment God extends to you.*

All the wonderful things God said about you in Psalm 139 are exactly how He feels about you now, even while you are in the process of persevering. If you feel anxious and impatient while waiting for your healing, remember that He loves you very much, and never leaves or forsakes you. Persevere. He is with you.

Because God loves you, He doesn't just want you to survive; He wants you to experience the joy of living! God's prophet, Isaiah, said it this way: "To all who mourn in Israel, he will give beauty for ashes, joy instead of mourning, praise instead of despair. For the LORD has planted them like strong and graceful oaks for his own glory" (Isa. 61:3 NLT).

TOUGH REALITY

There are times, when persevering, that you get discouraged. You are only human. It feels like you can't take any more. You've waited and waited. You finally take two steps forward, only to take three steps back.

One day you sense that you might be healing, only to experience two days of misery. Healing seems like a distant promise.

You're losing confidence in persevering and wondering if other options might work quicker. There are plenty of false options awaiting you: drugs, illicit relationships, gambling, co-dependent friends and more. However, you know that is not the answer.

All this is made worse because you feel a sense of guilt. Did you bring all this on yourself? Will you ever recover? How long can you persevere? Can you possibly heal?

Then reality hits you hard. There are no quick fixes or easy solutions. You can't take a shortcut. You would never consider taking your life, but you are very tempted to run for your life!

Will you run? Will you give up the healing process and succumb to some easy solution—one that will make you sicker?

No! You will face your tough reality and plow through it! God will give you the necessary strength. Jesus will persevere with you, because He promised never to leave or forsake you. The Holy Spirit will guide you, so make the tough choice to persevere. Now is not the time to run! If you run now, you run away from God's will. Instead, take the practical advice of Scripture, "Those who endure to the end will be saved" (Matt. 24:13 NLT). You have come too far in your healing to give up now. Christianity is a distance run, not a sprint. It takes patience and perseverance.

Confucius once told his students something very important. He said, "It does not matter how slowly you go, so long as you do not stop."

A MATTER OF TRUST

There is a human trait in us that begins working when we face problems and crises. That trait is the tendency to solve our own problems. We are "wired up" to "fix" what isn't working properly. We're natural problem solvers. To be sure, some folks have not nurtured that trait as well as others, but it's still there in us.

Our problem-solving capacity is often hindered by our arrogance and naiveté. Problems arise and we think, *I'll take care of this. No problem!* In short order, we realize that we're in over our heads, and failing in our efforts to solve the problem.

At other times, problems arise and we think, *This is easy. Anybody could solve this!* Later, we find ourselves baffled by the perplexity of it.

We repeatedly fail at problem solving, yet still hold to the notion that we can handle whatever challenges us!

We move stubbornly through life thinking we're in control and can manage our own lives, when most of the time we have very little control.

However, if *Healing Is a Choice* teaches us anything, it is that we don't manage our lives very well. We damage one another. We experience considerable failure. We tolerate lifelong pain with no real plan for recovery. Our problem-solving ability is not as good as we imagined.

The apostle Paul spoke to this issue in 1 Corinthians. Using paradoxical language, he quickly catches our attention. Let's look at the text in several translations:

1. *Read 1 Corinthians 1:25–29 in two or three translations of your choice. Include the New International Version.*

2. *Now, read the New Living Translation printed below:*

Remember, dear brothers and sisters, that few of you were wise in the world's eyes, or powerful, or wealthy when God called you. Instead, God deliberately chose things the world considers foolish in order to shame those who think they are wise. And he chose those who are powerless to shame those who are powerful. God chose things despised by the world, things counted as nothing at all, and used them to bring to nothing what the world considers important, so that no one can ever boast in the presence of God. (1 Cor. 1:26–29)

Reading several translations gives you a good sense of the paradox Paul describes.

We imagine ourselves to be great problem solvers. We think we are smart, but what we consider smart, God often views as foolish. What God considers wise, we often view as foolish.

A good biblical example is Namaan (2 Kin. 5:1–14). He was a decent man who had been stricken with leprosy. King Aram loved him and sought help from the Israelite prophet Elisha. The prophet sent word to Namaan, instructing him to do something unexpected and seemingly foolish. Elisha's message was, "Go wash yourself seven times in the Jordan River, and you will be healed." Initially, Namaan was offended. It made no sense to him. Why bath in the muddy Jordan, when two other beautiful rivers were accessible to him? It must have felt like an insult to a man of Namaan's stature.

However, God's ways are paradoxical and unexpected. When we think we're being smart, God says it's foolish. Namaan thought the instructions were foolish. God called it wisdom. Namaan swallowed his pride and dunked himself in the muddy little river, seven times!

It must have wounded his pride. How would his fellow soldiers and servants react? What would happen to his reputation when word reached home regarding this indignity?

Namaan thought it through very carefully. What if the prophet was right? What if he could be healed? Was Elisha's God that powerful? What if he bathed in the river and nothing happened?

In the end, Namaan made a powerful healing decision. He admitted to those around him, but mostly to himself, that he was ill and could not heal himself. He persevered. He didn't run for his horse and ride away angry. He may not have been thrilled with the prescription Elisha gave him, but he slowly squatted, lower and lower, until he was underwater. He came up. No change! He persevered. One down, six to go!

The seventh time up, he was healed. He rose above his pride and persevered.

Namaan's choice to trust Elisha's God was a bold step for a pagan soldier. He realized he was not in control of his life. His only option was to trust, risk, and persevere.

Healing is also a matter of trust for us. Like Namaan, we want it on our terms, but that is not likely to be the way we will be healed. Our healing will be on God's terms. It may not make sense to you. It may even seem foolish, but it will be genuine healing. Sometimes, it takes a great deal of perseverance to reach the place where God can heal us. As we said earlier, God is in the persevering. He is working all things out for your good. Will you trust Him, or will you struggle to work out your own solutions?

NOT ALONE IN DOUBTS

Some years ago, Os Guinness wrote a wonderful and challenging book titled *In Two Minds*.[2] The subject of the book was doubt.

Too many well-meaning Christians have been taught that doubt is synonymous with unbelief. Nothing could be farther from the truth. Such teaching is particularly destructive to those struggling with healing.

God is never surprised or particularly offended by our doubts. Guinness suggests that doubt is the beginning of true faith. He also writes, "In no way is the fact that we doubt a negative reflection on our faith."

He explains a great truth about doubt: "Doubt is not so much our problem as everybody's problem. It is not primarily a Christian problem, but a human problem."

The truth is that we all struggle with doubt, and God understands that struggle. To have doubt is not synonymous with denying our faith, but it is to acknowledge our humanity.

Many people in the Bible struggled with doubts of various kinds, but God did not reject them. Most of us struggle with doubt, and, thankfully, God does not reject us.

Go back and read the story of Gideon in chapter 9. Gideon was demoralized and asked the angel of the Lord, "If the Lord is with us, why has all this happened to us?" and "Where are the miracles our ancestors told us about?" It would not be surprising to discover that most Christians have asked those two questions at some point in their lives. Many of the people mentioned in this book wrestle with those questions every day! "Why has this happened to me?" and "Where are the miracles that could end my suffering?" In the absence of an answer, doubt is a normal human response.

Gideon had plenty of doubts, and probably a good supply of fears, but he went to battle. The point is that Gideon was not disqualified by God simply because he had some doubts. God is not afraid of our doubts. He is patient and understanding of our human struggles. As a result, we can persevere!

A bright person once offered this observation: "Show me a person with no doubts, and I will show you a person drowning in denial!" That is not great oratory, but it is great truth. To be human is to struggle with doubt to some degree.

The notion that doubt is "un-Christian" is particularly destructive, and even cruel for those who suffer.

Frankly, those who say they have no doubts are being arrogant. It is important to remember that Thomas, the disciple, was a doubter. He spent three years in the presence of the Son of God, but after the Crucifixion, he doubted the Resurrection.

Scripture reminds us that many of the disciples deserted Jesus. From our perspective, that's hard to imagine. We judge those men and think, *How could they?!* Didn't they remember the miracles? Didn't they recall His words? How could they doubt? The truth is, they did just what you and I have done. They doubted!

Here is an important truth. The problem with doubt is not that we waver in our Christian fidelity. The problem is that it attacks our ability to persevere. Doubt is like a roadblock, stopping us smack in the middle of the road! It diverts our attention and hinders our progress.

Our goal is not to deny that we have doubts. Rather, it is to deal with them directly. We must acknowledge that we have doubt. The truth is that everybody has doubts of some sort, especially in times of weakness and pain. Having doubts is not an insurmountable barrier. Take the power out of doubts by diminishing them. Acknowledge it and move on. At all costs, persevere.

Please understand that your relationship with God is not predicated on doubts you may have. On the contrary, it is based entirely on the work of Jesus Christ on the cross for you!

The truth is graceful. You can trust in Christ, even as you wrestle with doubts of various kinds, and that is not a contradiction in terms!

IT REALLY WILL BE OKAY

Life is sometimes a very difficult taskmaster. Consider what happens when there are problems or crises in our lives. Some event occurs, often a painful one. There is an outcome on the horizon. What we have to endure is the awful period between the event and the outcome. That period can be an excruciating, painful, anxiety-ridden time. We desperately yearn for resolution, but it is not to be. Each crisis has its own timeline.

We cannot speed it up or slow it down. So, we wait and wring our hands worrying. We pace the floor. Then, in its own good time the resolution comes. We breathe a sigh of relief. It's over. And, the best part is that it worked out okay. Everything is going to be all right.

How many hours do we spend worrying about things that work out fine in the end? Part of our pain and worry results from trying to figure things out ourselves. We want to control the outcome, but that will not happen. We lack that control.

On the other hand, the apostle Paul offered a way of dealing with these tough moments: "And we know that God causes everything to work together for the good of those who love God and are called according to his purpose for them" (Rom. 8:28 NLT).

Between the events and the outcomes of life, we can trust that God is at work on our behalf. He is orchestrating the affairs of our lives so the outcomes will be for our good.

A believer's life does not unfold in a random way. It unfolds according to God's purposes. That is one of the most comforting truths in our lives. We are not alone. We are connected to Christ. He knows our pain, helps us face it, and is instrumental in our healing. He searches our hearts and helps us investigate our lives. He stands with us in our grief and strengthens us to make healing choices. He redeems our failures and gives us hope and the power to forgive.

Because God is attached to us, we know that regardless of what we face, everything really will be okay.

Even our pain and suffering are important, because they push us toward being okay. *Healing Is a Choice* reminds us: "Tough times make way for God's glory."

We all experience trouble, more often than we prefer. We worry about outcomes that result from the events in our lives. We hate the long, painful time between events and outcomes. But we know that God is with us, and "our present troubles are quite small and won't last very long. Yet they produce for us an immeasurably great glory that will last forever!" (2 Cor. 4:17 NLT).

Our response is simple. We must persevere! Never give up! Never, never give up.

Keep trusting! Keep believing! Keep enduring! Keep persevering!

THE TENTH BIG LIE:

"There is no hope for me."

King David had the perfect response to the tenth big lie. He wrote, "But as for me, I will always have hope; I will praise you more and more" (Ps. 71:14 NIV).

The theme of this chapter is the choice to persevere. Our perseverance needs motivation to keep us moving forward. Hope motivates us to persevere. Hope inspires us to keep making healing choices.

The tenth lie is vicious and cruel. It says, "You're worthless." "You're not worth God's time or attention." "Give up; you'll never heal." "Don't pay any attention to this book; it's all a pipe dream." "You're being set up!"

That lie tempts you to give up and settle for a life of pain and defeat. If you believe the lie, you will lose ground you fought long and hard to gain. This lie will add more pain and misery to your life. Even if you are struggling to maintain hope, remember that God has confidence in you. Please, at all costs, reject this lie!

REVIEW AND ACTION PLAN

You made an important decision to read *Healing Is a Choice*. You have gained the information necessary for your growth and healing. However, you need to stay invested in the healing process. This last exercise asks you to evaluate where you are now and create an action plan to guide you in the months ahead.

1. *The Choice to Connect Your Life. Check the one area below that best identifies where you are in the healing process now.*

   Still Struggling ____   Experiencing Success ____

   Making Progress ____   Feeling the Healing ____

   ACTION

   During the next six months, I will connect with more people by:

   a. _____

   b. _____

   c. _____

   ### THE BIG LIE:
   "All I need to heal is just God and me." Explain why this is a lie.

   _____

   _____

   _____

2. *The Choice to Feel Your Life. Check the one area below that best identifies where you are in the healing process now.*

Still Struggling ____   Experiencing Success ____

Making Progress ____   Feeling the Healing ____

ACTION

During the next six months, I will face the pains in my life, examine them, and deal with them by:

a. _____

b. _____

c. _____

THE BIG LIE:
"Real Christians should have real peace in all circumstances."

Explain why this is a lie.

_____

_____

_____

3. *The Choice to Investigate Your Life in Search of Truth. Check the one area below that best identifies where you are in the healing process now.*

Still Struggling ____   Experiencing Success ____

Making Progress ____   Feeling the Healing ____

ACTION

During the next six months, I will continue to investigate my life by:

a. _____

b. _____

c. _____

THE BIG LIE:
"All I need to heal is just God and me."

Explain why this is a lie.

_____

_____

_____

4. *The Choice to Heal Your Future. Check the one area below that best identifies where you are in the healing process now.*

Still Struggling ____   Experiencing Success ____

Making Progress ____   Feeling the Healing ____

ACTION

During the next six months, I will grieve the losses in my life, so that I can move boldly into the future by:

a. _____

b. _____

c. _____

THE BIG LIE:
"Time heals all wounds."

Explain why this is a lie.

_____

_____

_____

5. *The Choice to Help Your Life. Check the one area below that best identifies where you are in the healing process now.*

Still Struggling ____   Experiencing Success ____

Making Progress ____   Feeling the Healing ____

ACTION

During the next six months, I will make choices that contribute to my healing by:

a. _____

b. _____

c. _____

THE BIG LIE:

"I can figure this out by myself."

Explain why this is a lie.

_____

_____

_____

_____

6. *The Choice to Embrace Your Life. Check the one area below that best identifies where you are in the healing process now.*

Still Struggling ____   Experiencing Success ____

Making Progress ____   Feeling the Healing ____

ACTION

During the next six months, I will embrace and value my life
by:

a. _____

b. _____

c. _____

The Big Lie:

"If I just act as if there is no problem, it will finally go away."

Explain why this is a lie.

_____

_____

_____

7. *The Choice to Forgive. Check the one area below that
   best identifies where you are in the healing process now.*

   Still Struggling ____   Experiencing Success ____
   Making Progress ____   Feeling the Healing ____

ACTION

During the next six months, I will forgive people I have hurt,
or who have hurt me, by:

a. _____

b. _____

c. _____

THE BIG LIE:

"Forgiveness is only for those who deserve it or earn it."

Explain why this is a lie.

_____

_____

_____

8. *The Choice to Risk Your Life. Check the one area below that best identifies where you are in the healing process today.*

Still Struggling ____   Experiencing Success ____

Making Progress ____   Feeling the Healing ____

ACTION

During the next six months, I will take some healing risks.

a. _____

b. _____

c. _____

THE BIG LIE:

"I must protect myself from any more pain."

Why is that a lie?

_____

_____

_____

9. *The Choice to Serve. Check the one area below that best identifies where you are in the healing process today.*

Still Struggling _____   Experiencing Success _____
Making Progress _____   Feeling the Healing _____

ACTION
During the next six months, I will find ways to serve others by:

a. _____

b. _____

c. _____

THE BIG LIE:
"Until I am completely healed and strong, there is no place for me to serve God."

Explain why this is a lie.

_____

_____

_____

10. *The Choice to Persevere. Check the one area below that best identifies where you are in the healing process today.*

Still Struggling _____   Experiencing Success _____
Making Progress _____   Feeling the Healing _____

ACTION

During the next six months, I will commit myself to persevere in my healing efforts by:

a. _____

b. _____

c. _____

THE BIG LIE:

"There is no hope for me."

Explain why this is a lie.

_____

_____

_____

JOURNALING

You have made great progress in your healing journey. You have learned some important truths and gained valuable information from *Healing Is a Choice*. You have also faced some very dangerous lies that can undermine your healing. Now you have the opportunity to look back and measure your growth.

Use your journaling time to summarize your reactions to the book. Note its greatest strengths. List some of the things that you found most helpful. What information from the book will you share with others? Has reading the book changed you in significant ways? If so, how?

How has the Holy Spirit spoken to you during this study? Explain.

PRAYER

God of Grace, Mercy, and Healing, I thank You for giving me this book, Healing Is a Choice. *I have been challenged and changed by it. At times it has been hard to face the truth. Some hard choices remain in front of me. Through it all, I thank You for Your constant presence. You have never left me. You have given me reasons to have hope again. I have experienced the constant presence of the Holy Spirit, standing with me in this study. I will be healed, because You have shown me the way. How can I ever thank You? I don't have the words. But, I will praise and worship You. You are the God who loves me, and I love You. Bless others, I pray, who have studied this book and learned these truths. Heal them as You are healing me. Forgive my sins and guide me by Your loving hand. Give me strength to persevere. Through Christ, my Rock and Salvation, amen.*

NOTES

CHAPTER 2

1. *The American Heritage® Dictionary of the English Language*, Fourth Edition. Copyright © 2000 by Houghton Mifflin Company. Published by Houghton Mifflin Company. All rights reserved.

CHAPTER 4

1. William Shakespeare, *The Tempest* (Antonio at II, i).

CHAPTER 5

1. W. W. Norton, *Norton Anthology of English Literature*, 5th Ed., "Devotions Upon Emergent Occasions," Meditation 17, 1962, Vol. 1, 1107.

CHAPTER 7

1. *American Heritage® Dictionary*.
2. K.A. Lawler, J.W. Younger, R.L. Piferi, et al. "A change of heart: cardiovascular correlates of forgiveness in response to cardiovascular fitness.," *Journal of Behavioral Medicine*, October 2003:26(5), pp. 373–93.

CHAPTER 8

1. L. Frank Baum, *The Wonderful World of Oz* (Chicago: George M. Hill, 1900).

CHAPTER 9

1. Ruth Bell Graham, *Legacy of a Pack Rat* (Nashville: Thomas Nelson, 1994).

2. Richard Foster, *Celebration of Discipline* (Harper: San Francisco, 1988), 113.

3. Henri Nouwen, *The Wounded Healer* (New York: Random House, 1979).

CHAPTER 10

1. Thomas E. Dipko, "Believing Against the Odds," *Clergy Journal*.

2. Os Guinness, *In Two Minds* (Downers' Grove, Ill., InterVarsity Press, 1976), 39–40.